INTERNATIONAL
BEACH HOUSES

LOUISA WATTSON

ABRAMS, NEW YORK

EUROPE

NORTH AMERICA

SOUTH AMERICA

THE HOUSE

For every society throughout human history, the house has been the most important architectural object. It offers shelter, both physical and psychological, and is an expression of who we are and how we live.

Today, in a world that is becoming increasingly globalized, the house continues to hold its same importance. And for some, who have greater means, a capacity for change, and ease of transportation, the house has also become a place of escape from more urban surroundings, a way to inhabit other places, if even for no more than a few days.

These twenty-three houses have also become symbols of another way in which we inhabit space.

ARCHITECTURE AND LOCATION

Whether located in a public or private area, open or closed to its environment, the house, at its best, represents through its construction the emotional and symbolic make-up of its inhabitants and is conditioned by the particular time and place it occupies. When this fails to happen, a sameness of structure often occurs that inevitably dilutes the relationship between man and nature. Each house in this book, however, represents a successful example of "habitable architecture."

THE "NATURE" OF THE SEA

For contemporary man, developing harmony with nature is as complex as it is necessary. In our ever-changing world, we contemplate and enjoy natural spaces unspoiled by the actions of man, but they are still landscapes occupied by man himself—except for "empty" seascapes, which continue to transport us into the air, the light, and, above all, into uninterrupted harmony with nature.

IN THIS BOOK

From six continents, twenty-three houses have been chosen, with the intention of showing a diversity of formal responses to the challenge presented in constructing a house next to water. Situated on the shores of seas, oceans, or great lakes, the houses respond to climatic and cultural conditions as well as ever more convergent architectural traditions, and with their harmonious relationship to their surroundings, they represent an inspiring collection of "good" works of architecture.

COROMANDEL BEACH HOUSE

Crosson Clarke Architects | Coromandel Peninsula, New Zealand | PHOTOGRAPHER: PATRICK REYNOLDS

Dominating a solitary corner on the paradisiacal Coromandel Peninsula, this holiday home with its "Let's get back to nature" style has been planned to bring life into direct contact with the natural surroundings from which contemporary man is becoming increasingly removed. To confront this fact, and in response to the desire of their clients, Crosson Clarke Architects have constructed this house in which "quiet time spent in a calm place allows us to enjoy the small things of life." This aspect, along with the absence of televisions, computers, and dishwashers, stimulates their clients to "connect with the basic things of life."

. The anthropological desire to "get back to nature" has been directly translated into the architectural aspects of this house, which

is based on traditional New Zealand architecture (strongly related to the rural life of the first colonizers), and which preserves the essence of "craftsmanship in the woodwork, in which the structure, coverings, finishes, and carpentry are expressed in a way that is unrefined and clear." All of this gives rise to a wooden container lightly set in its place, a "hut that connects with nature and with the natural," and that opens up onto the virgin landscape lapped by the waters of the Pacific Ocean.

By means of a simple electric mechanism, the "box" opens up upon the clients' arrival and two attached surfaces unfold, on which life in the open air can be enjoyed. These terraces disappear to "protect" the residence when the volume is closed.

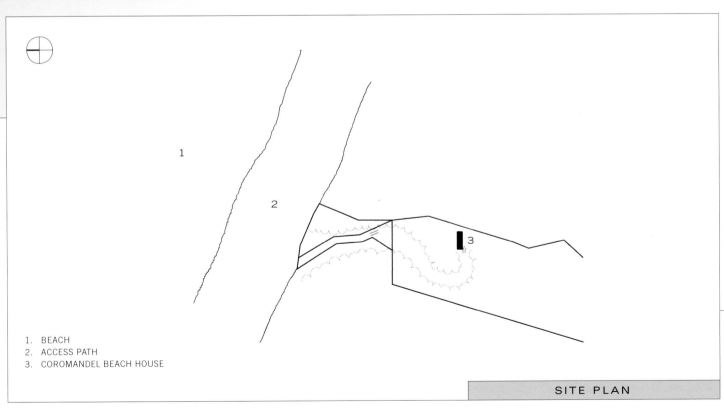

1. BEACH
2. ACCESS PATH
3. COROMANDEL BEACH HOUSE

SITE PLAN

The house, a wooden box of "renewable and sustainable material," is situated on the ridge of a hill near Coromandel Beach and overlooks the coast while facing north from an area free of the bushes that surround it. It consists of just one floor and is reached along a path that comes up from the beach and ends at the southern facade. When the box is open—on the opposing northern side—the resulting wooden surface provides access to the living/dining area, the large central space of the house that opens up onto the landscape from the wooden extension converted into terraces. Around this central space are the other rooms. These are the parents' bedroom and principal bathroom on the east side of the house, and the guest room, the lavatory, and the children's rooms on the west side. As a result, the children's rooms are cool because they are relatively enclosed, but the other bedrooms, the living room, and the bathroom are open—to say the least—to the exterior and to the sun. Among these spaces, the bathroom stands out, not only because it opens onto the outside, but also because of a movable bathtub that converts the rituals of showering and bathing into experiences linked to nature.

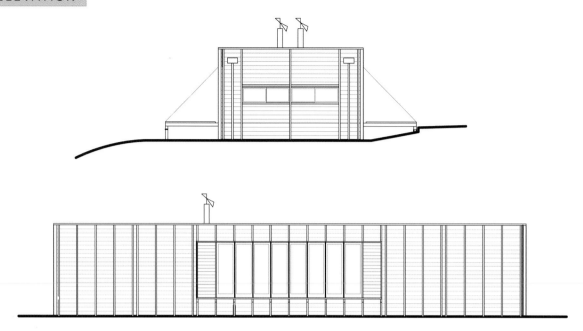

1. ENTRANCE
2. LIVING / DINING AREA / KITCHEN
3. BEDROOM
4. TERRACE
5. STOREROOM / SERVICE

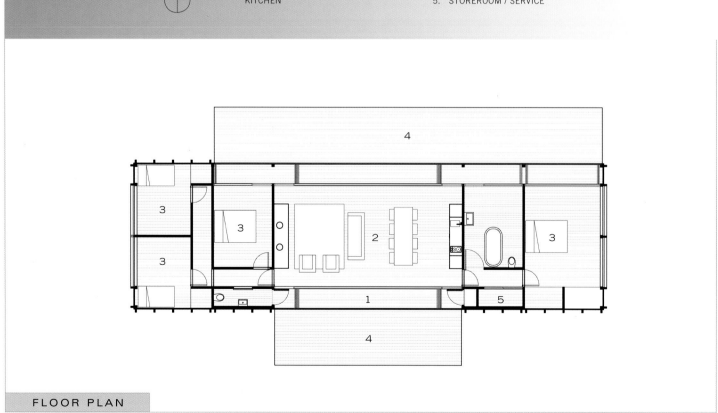

FLOOR PLAN

The house is made entirely of wood, which was used in the structure as well as in the exterior sidings, the interior finishes, the carpentry of the windows, and all of the furniture.

Along with the chimney and glazing, the wood's thermal insulation capacity is extended in the form of screens that can be opened or closed, allowing the residence to be used during the winter months of the year.

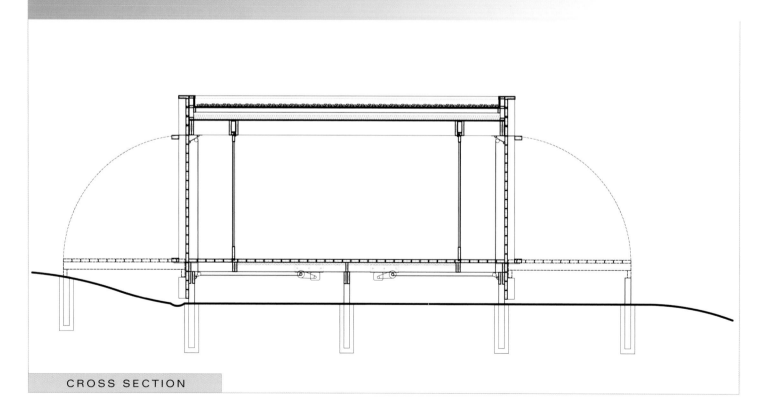

CROSS SECTION

"This house was intended to provide, within the natural landscape, a place that captures the essence of vacation spirit in New Zealand."

SHARK ALLEY RESIDENCE

Fearon Hay Architects | Medlands Bay, Great Barrier Island, New Zealand | PHOTOGRAPHER: PATRICK REYNOLDS

Just before the southern limits of Medlands Bay, the fascinating landscape of the Great Barrier Island, made up of a succession of green valleys and pronounced hills, reaches a gradient that descends toward a beach called Shark Alley, which slides into the Pacific Ocean. Here, amidst the dense greenery of manuka trees and pastures, Fearon Hay Architects constructed a house based on the ideal of "escaping from solid land" while capturing all of the energy of the virgin landscape by means of "solid architecture in which to comfortably take shelter from the solitary and aggressive surroundings." They were given the freedom to choose the best site for the house within a sixteen-acre plot and decided to situate it on the point where a steep hill becomes a smooth plane on its descent to the sea, orienting it to the north.

From this position, which controls the landscape, a patio was created between the hill and the house in the form of an "L" that is open to the exterior. Through a system of sliding doors, the public spaces of the residence enjoy a close relationship to the patio and surrounding landscape. The degree to which the windows are opened can be regulated at all times according to the temperature and breezes. This allows the whole house to be a rational architectural object that is inserted into the location as a form of malleable abstraction.

The residence is planned to facilitate a life that is in contact with the warm, virgin environment, and thus the patio adopts the role of exterior space controlled by and incorporated into the residence. The whole house is one height, set upon a floor plan in the form of an "L" that pivots on the patio and provides, along the length of the perimeter of this exterior space, as much access to the residence as a complete interior circular route.

Directly off the patio, on the short side of the "L," we find a storeroom and the kitchen pantry, spatially united to the living/dining room, situated on the longer side of the "L." At the end of the patio, next to a bathroom and a lavatory, are two of the four bedrooms of the house. The two remaining bedrooms and a bathroom parallel these, but in another independent body situated between the principal volume, the hill, and the patio.

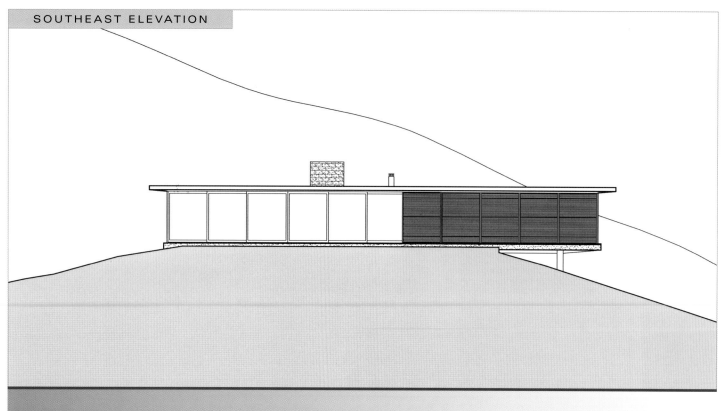

1. ENTRANCE
2. PATIO

3. LIVING / DINING ROOM
4. KITCHEN

5. BEDROOM
6. SERVICE / STOREROOM

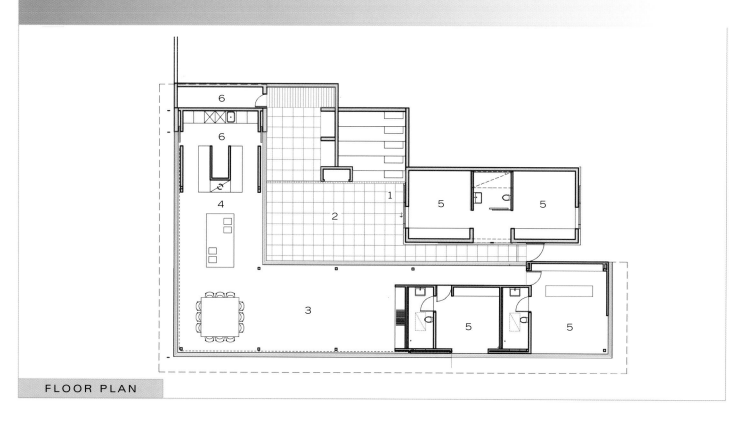

FLOOR PLAN

The entire house can be synthesized as a large horizontal plane at rest on the slope that supports it, on which part of the structure is suspended and part is excavated into the hillside. On top of this large plane lies the main volume, the body containing the bedrooms and the empty space of the patio.

Alongside the exterior concrete paving, poured in situ, the patio consists of bare concrete blocks and prefabricated concrete slabs, which together make up an exterior space that is at once abstract and solid and clearly articulates the entire house.

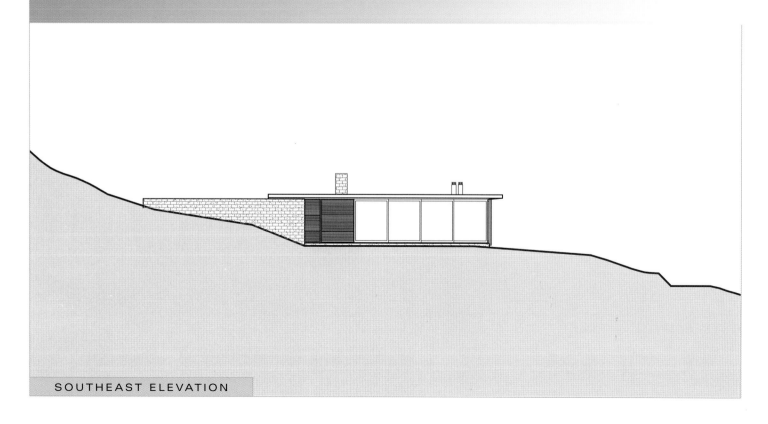

SOUTHEAST ELEVATION

Over the large slab of steel-reinforced concrete set out over the plot, a lightness in the volumes was sought, seen in the use of metal doorways and large openings, with windows and sliding blinds forming a second skin of mobile elements that allow for a "great flexibility in controlling shade, privacy, and ventilation, as well as the views and the protection" of the interior spaces of the house.

GLEDHILL HOUSE

Tanner Architects | New South Wales, Australia | PHOTOGRAPHER: RICHARD GLOVER [VIEW]

The east coast of Australia is constantly dotted by a sequence of entrances and projections in the form of points and small bays containing sandy beaches which, when they fall within the reach of the ocean, have come to form harbors. At the head of one of these entrances, called Boat Harbour, looking toward a small sandy beach surrounded by vegetation molded by the ocean winds, is this holiday home constructed by Tanner Architects. Thanks to a carefully developed project, they have managed to successfully capture, with sensitivity, the intense light of the sun, frame the views of the virgin landscape that surrounds the house, and visually eliminate the presence of the neighboring homes. The architects designed the house for a respected builder with whom they had previously worked on larger-scale projects and on another holiday home, also situated within the area of Port Stephens. This extensive professional relationship facilitated the daring architectural language and secured the quality of the resulting construction.

This house makes the most of the site's possibilities, which, "with its warm climate and exceptional situation for the practice of all sorts of open-air activities, offers a unique opportunity for the development of a contemporary architectural language that facilitates life in contact with the outdoors."

Inside this rectangular plot, inclined softly toward the sea, the house has been distributed in a functional sense over two floors, which led to the creation of "two compartments, with the parents using the upper floor throughout the year as a second residence, while the lower floor is only used in summer by the now-adult children

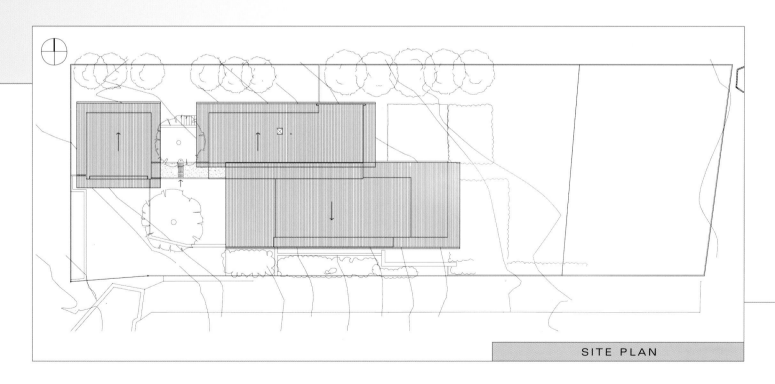

accompanied by their respective families." This functional division is expressed in terms of construction when it comes to comparing the lower floor, built in solidly rendered brickwork, with the apparently floating upper floor constructed in metal, glass, and wood. Based on the separation of functions already described, situated on the upper floor are: the living/dining room, a kitchen area, the principal bedroom, a guest room, a bathroom, a garage, and a patio, through which the house is accessed. The lower floor was constructed by making the most of the plot's existent gradient and accommodates a large

playroom/bedroom for the grandchildren that opens onto the garden and is surrounded by the children's bedrooms.

The exterior spaces play a fundamental role in the layout of the house because they are living areas in which all sorts of open-air activities can be carried out. On the upper floor, the roof has been extended to protect the suspended terrace, while at the opposite end of the living room we find the patio protected from the wind. On the lower floor, a covered terrace opens onto the garden, which leads to the beach.

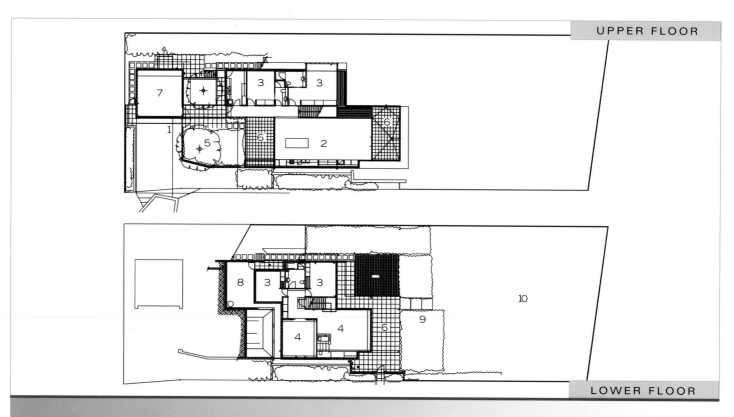

1. ENTRANCE
2. LIVING / DINING ROOM /
   KITCHEN
3. BEDROOM
4. PLAYROOM /
   BEDROOM
5. PATIO
6. TERRACE
7. GARAGE
8. STOREROOM /
   SERVICE
9. GARDEN
10. BEACH

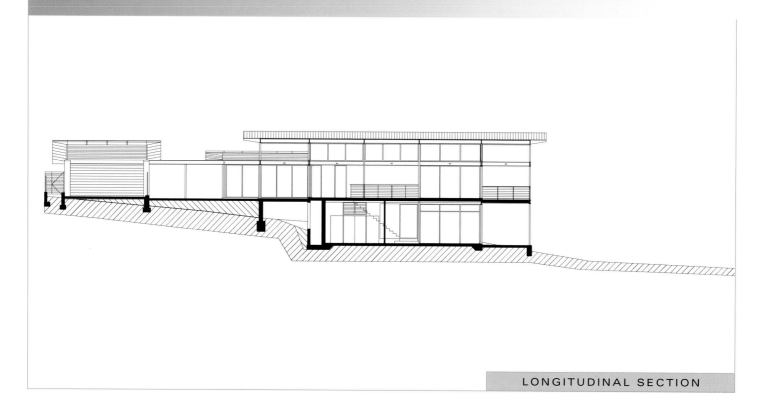

LONGITUDINAL SECTION

The dialogue between the lightly inclined metal roofing and the severe vertical forms of the walls, rendered in a light color, gives strength and simplicity to the whole. This is expressed by the solid base of the brick walls of the lower floor and the finishes in metal on the upper floor. Anticorrosion protection of all the metal elements used in the house has been carefully taken into account.

PICTURE WINDOW HOUSE

Shigeru Ban Architects | Shizuoka, Japan | PHOTOGRAPHER: HIROYUKI HYRAI

Going in a northerly direction and climbing up from the sea a few hundred meters over a hill on the Izu Peninsula, Shigeru Ban found "a place free from distraction" in which to construct a house. The views of the never-ending horizon and its elevated position—close to the top of the hill—create a visual relationship with the ocean as the main spatial and compositional arguments of the house, which itself is an abstract architectural object superimposed on this particular site. Shigeru Ban explains this in the following way: "The first time I put a foot on this place, my immediate response was to frame the marvelous views of the ocean by stretching them horizontally. This meant that the building itself would become a window. Also, to prevent the architecture from becoming an obstacle that altered the sensation that the place flows from the ocean, I decided to keep the continuity by having it run through the building up to the trees situated at the top of the hill. As a result, the top floor became an enormous beam that forms the upper part of a twenty-meter window."

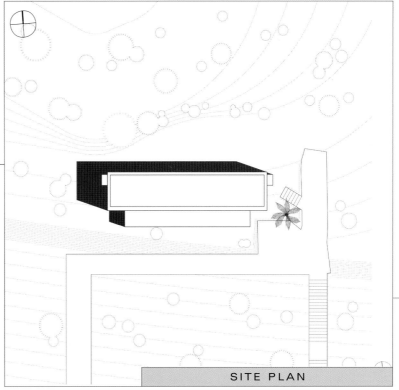

SITE PLAN

The rectangular floor plan of the house, for structural and compositional reasons, is made up of three differentiated parts: the central (with its twenty meters of light and views) and two lateral parts that contain the supporting structure. Shigeru Ban successfully avoided the rigidity imposed by the structural scheme in the way he distributed the house and achieved a certain degree of experimentation.

Access to the house is on the side of the building and is formed by a double-height hall, which, along with the bathroom, makes up the lower floor of one of the "structural" sides. These elements facilitate the openness as well as the cleanness of the central part of the residence where all of the public spaces are concentrated. This area contains the living room, the dining room, the kitchen, and the main staircase. On the side opposite from the entrance is the studio, which has its own staircase since it also occupies the first floor. In the central part of this floor, from which the sea can be seen through a luminous screen, are the four bedrooms. Behind these, open to the top of the hill and grouped within a single space interrupted by no more than glass divisions, are the staircase, the bathrooms, and the entrance doors to the bedrooms. Finally, on the structural side, opposite the studio, are the dressing room that belongs to the master bedroom and the hall space.

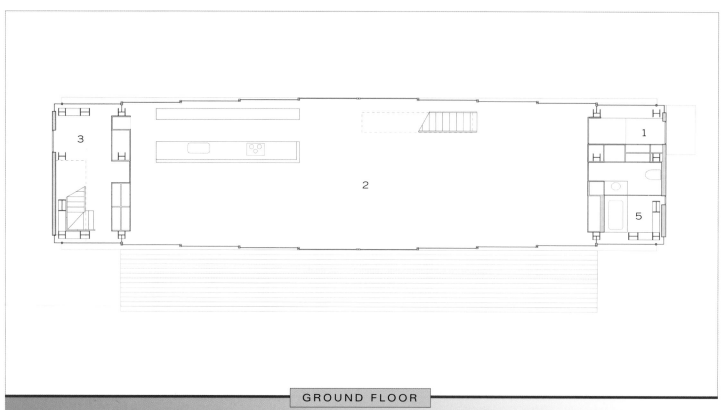

1. ENTRANCE
2. LIVING / DINING / KITCHEN AREA
3. STUDY
4. BEDROOM
5. BATHROOM
6. DRESSING ROOM
7. VOID

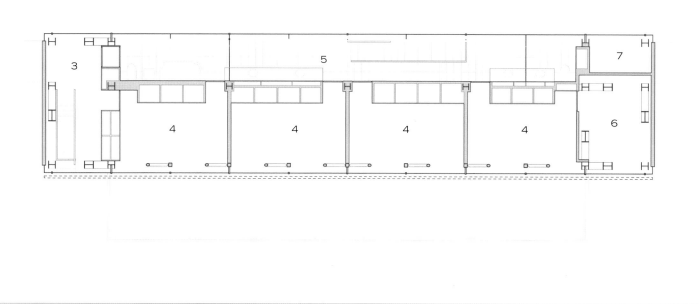

Protected from the southern sun by a lightweight canopy, the central part of the ground floor is free from any structural obligation since the entire house acts as a porch that is twenty meters wide.

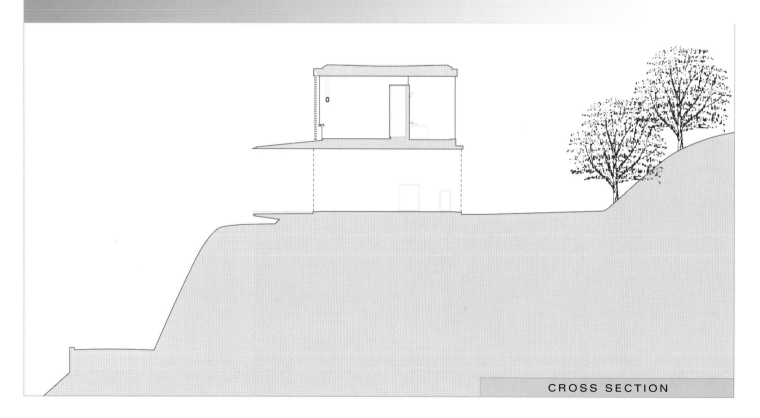

CROSS SECTION

On the first floor, the southern facade contains a triangular beam. This structural element can be appreciated from the outside through a series of horizontal slats which, as well as offering protection from the sun, act as a visual filter and give privacy to the bedrooms.

The other large supporting beam is in line with the partition wall that separates the bedrooms from the surprising adjoining space and not only makes it possible for the northern facade to be freed structurally, but also allows the bathroom-passage-staircase to open completely toward the hilltop.

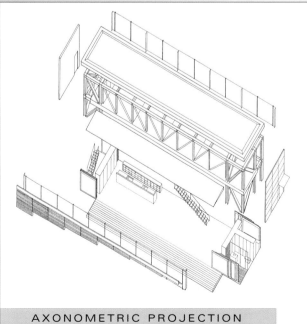

AXONOMETRIC PROJECTION

The entire house was constructed of prefabricated elements. Steel, aluminum, and glass envelop the wooden flooring, and the white prefabricated partition walls create a lightweight, abstract architectural object that, set in its place with great delicacy, exists in harmony with the place in which it was born and toward which it is directed.

4 x 4 HOUSE

Tadao Ando Architect & Associates | Kobe, Hyogo, Japan | PHOTOGRAPHER: MITSUO MATSUOKA

During the great earthquake in Hanshin in 1995, the entire world saw how Japan mobilized itself in the aftermath of a natural disaster and managed to efficiently organize the reconstruction of its damaged buildings and urban infrastructures. The epicenter of the earthquake was on Awaji Island, where various works by the architect Tadao Ando can be found. Among these, the Water Temple and the Yumebutai stand out.

Across from the island, on the Kobe coast, an area of wasteland lies between a beach of extraordinary beauty and some unsightly railway lines. The main quality of this place is not its immediate surroundings but the views it commands of the Seto Sea, Awaji Island,

and the Akashi Bridge, a symbol of Japanese civil engineering. On this complex site, Tadao Ando has built a lookout house that is closed off from its immediate inhospitable surroundings but open to the views in the distance. Because of its great height, it is a landmark in the landscape.

The four-story house was conceived over a four-by-four-meter floor plan where the top floor becomes a cube measuring four meters on each of its sides. This cube is offset by one meter to the south and one meter to the east in such a way as to constitute a brilliant formal resource which, from its underlying simplicity, creates a complex volume.

AERIAL VIEW

Due to its reduced useful surface area and the fact that the house was conceived as a high construction, only one function has been allocated to each floor. As a result, access to the different spaces has been established by means of a staircase that connects the four levels. The entrance, a lavatory, and the bathroom are on the ground floor. The bedroom is situated on the first floor. These two lower levels are closed off from the outside and the windows are no larger than necessary to illuminate the interior and preserve privacy. However, as we climb up to the higher floors, we discover the landscape through large openings. First, we find a studio, and then, on the top floor, the living/kitchen/dining area, where "the landscape seen from within the cube is a panoramic vision that includes the Seto Sea, Awaji Island, and Akashi Bridge, upon which, as much for the client as for me, thoughts and memories of the earthquake are encrusted."

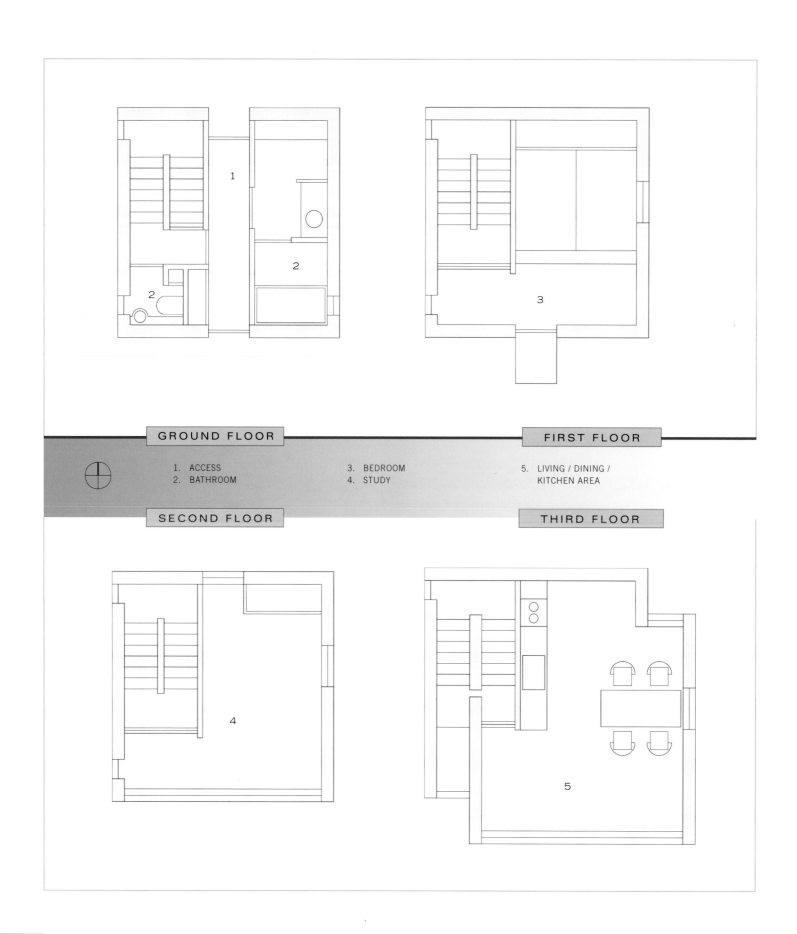

GROUND FLOOR

FIRST FLOOR

1. ACCESS
2. BATHROOM

3. BEDROOM
4. STUDY

5. LIVING / DINING /
   KITCHEN AREA

SECOND FLOOR

THIRD FLOOR

The house is constructed of steel-reinforced concrete walls built in situ. These walls, having been left uncovered, fulfill both structural and material functions. Throughout the interiors, the abstract gray textures are set off against the warmth of the wood used in the flooring and furniture.

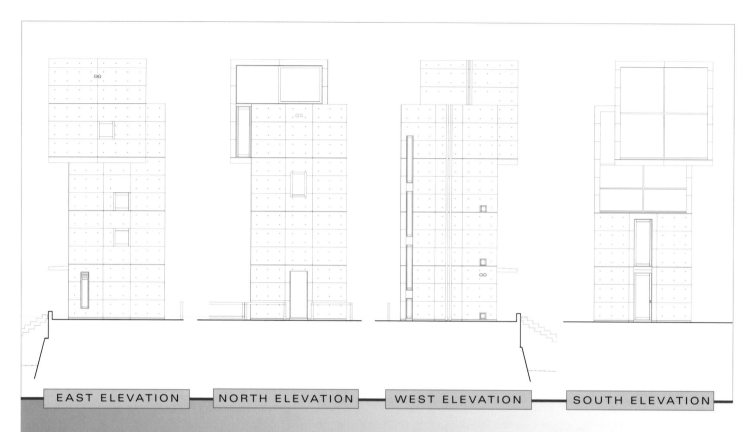

| EAST ELEVATION | NORTH ELEVATION | WEST ELEVATION | SOUTH ELEVATION |

The house appears closed off from its harsh immediate surroundings as it rises, enabling its occupants to contemplate only the Seto Sea.

CROSS SECTION

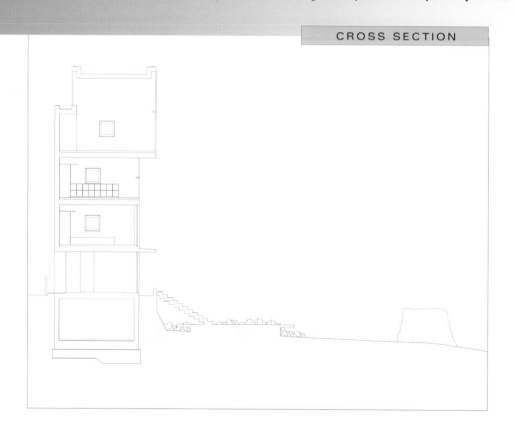

"I wish to model space with the delicate spirit of a craftsman. However, I have resolved to penetrate this space by the use of violence. I intend to impregnate the delicacy that has distinguished the Oriental world with intense originality."

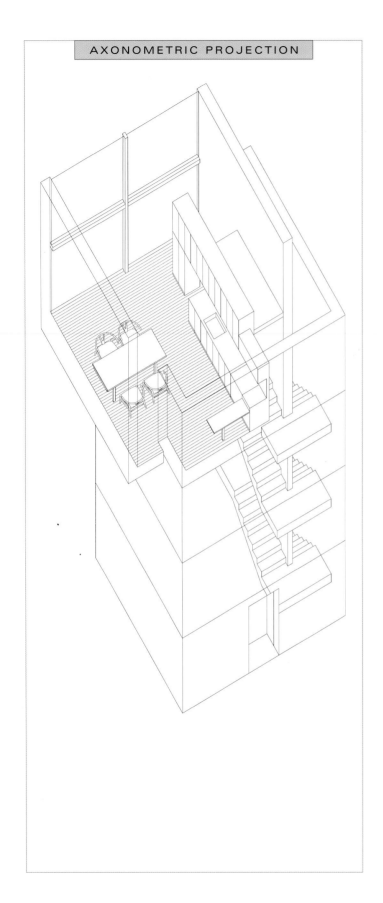

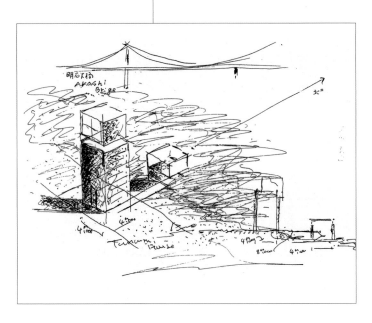

At present, there are plans to create an extension for this house, situated on the beach as if it were "architecture that breaches the water at high tide."

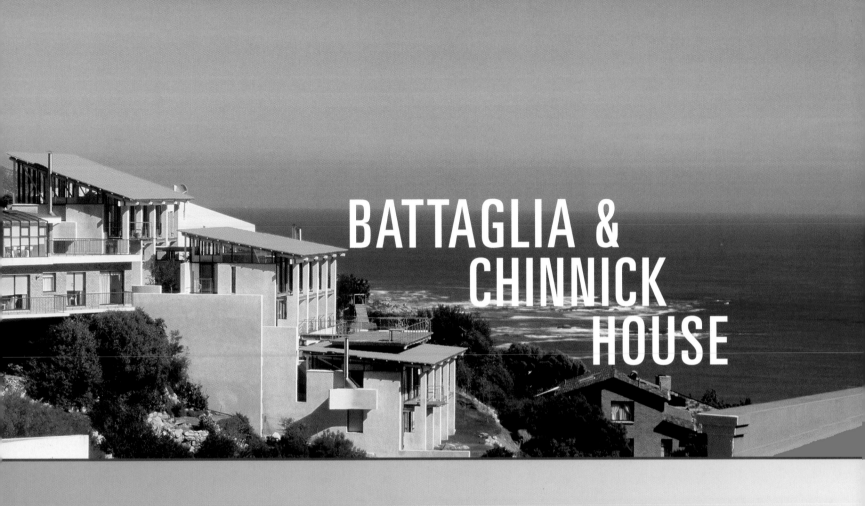

BATTAGLIA & CHINNICK HOUSE

Studio KrugerRoos | Camps Bay, Cape Town, South Africa | PHOTOGRAPHER: RONNIE LEVITAN

Camps Bay is a neighborhood in Cape Town made up of family homes that open onto the Atlantic Ocean from the privileged heights of the Twelve Apostles. One of the numerous mountain formations situated on the peninsula of the Cape of Good Hope, it is a mythical geographic situation; despite not being the most southerly point of the African continent (an honor reserved for Cape Agulhas), it has been, since its discovery by Bartolomeu Dias in the fifteenth century, the place where the oceans that surround Africa—the Atlantic and the Indian—symbolically meet. Here, in the extreme south of the multiracial city of Cape Town, on a plot with a severe gradient that overlooks the ocean from the Twelve Apostles, two European bankers of different origins and aesthetic sensitivities wished to construct a house that lent itself to the splendid views.

In response to these conditions, Studio KrugerRoos designed a house that would optimize the views of the mountains and of the ocean by arranging three pavilions at different heights on the gradient of the slope to make up a homogeneous but broken group composition in which the upper and lower pavilions would accommodate the private spaces of each of the clients and the intermediate area would be used for the shared public spaces. The house "has been structured in terraces that enclose patios and create balconies while locating the different functions on a series of steps." The three sections are finished with inclined roofs that continue the profile of the site, with the lower one having a reduced gradient to accommodate the large wooden surface area from which to look out over the ocean.

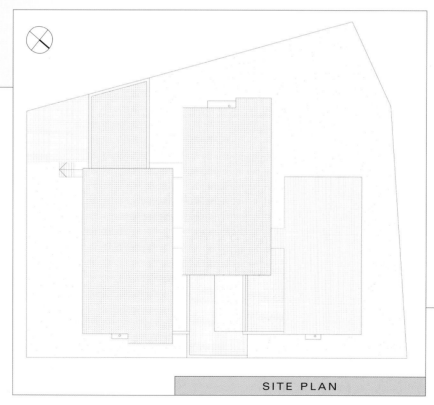

SITE PLAN

The spaces between the pavilions are occupied by various patios and terraces that help introduce natural light and space into the interiors that overlook the sea. The access is found in the upper part of the plot, where an open flight of steps leads down to the intermediate floor of the public pavilion. In this body, which has three floors, are found all of the house's public spaces, so that the other two pavilions can be dedicated to the private spaces of each client. Situated on the two upper floors of the public pavilion are the dining room, the kitchen, the informal living room, and the studio. Together these elements make up one space of double height, open on one side to the swimming pool and terrace, and on the other side to the large lookout terrace on the roof of the lower part. Descending from the high area by means of a staircase that passes next to the swimming

pool, the lower floor of the common space can be accessed. Here, the formal living room opens onto a garden situated in the bottom part of the plot. From this living room can be reached the garden and a patio, the lower pavilion, which accommodates the private spaces of one of the clients. This part consists of two floors on which the principal bedroom, library, and bathroom look out on the views from the upper floor of the double space, while below are two bedrooms, a living room, and a bathroom. This spatial arrangement is repeated exactly on the upper part to accommodate the private spaces of the other client and is accessed by means of a staircase that starts at the high area in the public pavilion. Cut off and separated by the entrance steps, the garage has been situated at the top of the highest space.

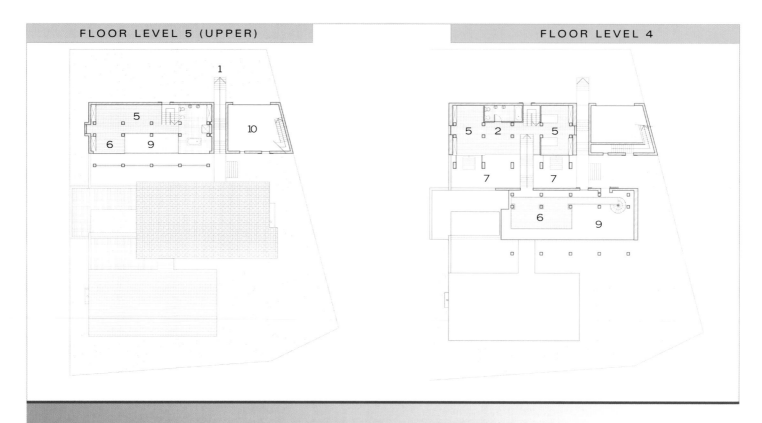

1. ENTRANCE
2. FORMAL LIVING ROOM
3. INFORMAL LIVING ROOM
4. KITCHEN
5. BEDROOM
6. STUDY
7. TERRACE
8. SWIMMING POOL
9. HOLLOW
10. GARAGE

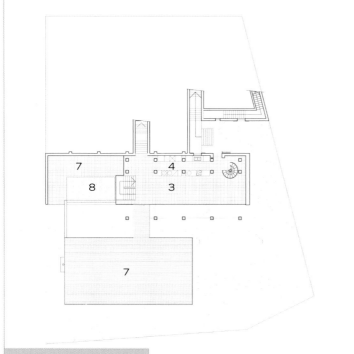

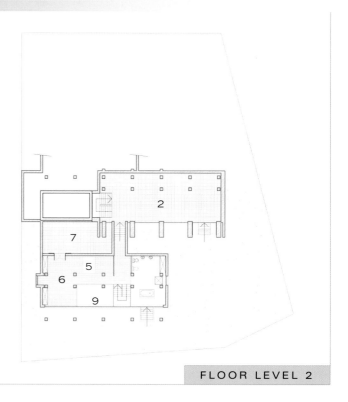

The structure of the house, a mixture of steel and concrete, dictates the layout of the inclined tiled roofs and white facades with large glazed areas.

"The roofs of this house, from which the views of the mountains and of the ocean can be enjoyed, echo the lay of the land as they follow its contours."

CROSS SECTION

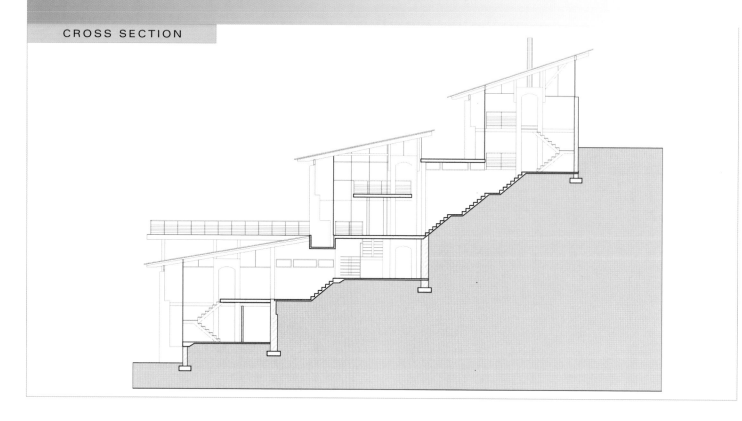

The interiors have been finished in white, which contrasts with the wood used for paving the interior as well as the exterior areas.

GUEST HOUSE

KHRAS arkitekter | Struer, Denmark | PHOTOGRAPHER: IB SORENSEN

The light, the strength of the spatial openings in the Toftum Bjerge cliff formation, and the clear blue skies of the Limfjord region inspired a large number of the works by the Danish artist Jens Sondergaard who, during the 1930s, went to live in a house in Toftum to paint those "marvelously extensive landscapes" that captivated his imagination. Set upon these very landscapes, on a pronounced gradient that looks out to sea, is the Guest House—executed by the Danish office KHRAS—which was established as an "autonomous extension" to the client's existing residence. It was conceived both as a complementary pavilion to the original house and as an independent residence for guests. The structure opens to a visual arc of more than 200° running from northeast to northwest. It

encompasses the pastures and dunes of the Nissum Bredning coast, a landscape that preserves much of its original beauty.

In response to the conditions of the place, the main objective was to capture the area's impressive views along with the sunlight, which shines on the side of the building opposite from that which commands the views. As a result, an abstract pavilion integrates into the landscape by means of its copper covering and basalt terraces, and leaves the interior a continual space that, although closed to the south, opens to the outside through a succession of openings to the east, north, and west and captures the southern light through a continuous window that wraps around the house.

The residence is based on one story and is completely open to the

1. MAIN HOUSE
2. GUEST HOUSE

SITE PLAN

exterior by means of the windows that run around the entire perimeter, with the exception of the southern facade, which presents a closed volume. The spatial continuity intended for the interior of the house is sustained by its functional flexibility, since the house can be used as an autonomous residence by guests, an office and bonsai garden, or for both uses at the same time.

To enable flexibility of function, the entrance to the residence can be established from either the eastern or western extreme because in both cases open terraces jut out beyond the volume of the building. These exterior surfaces are used during the day in accordance with the orientation of the sun and they limit the interior space that has been conceived as "a succession of continuous spaces." Within this succession, and located in an east–west direction, we find the client's office, the dining/living area, the bonsai room, the main bathroom, and the bedroom. All of the services of the house, such as the storage cupboards, installations, fireplace, kitchen, and lavatory, that together establish a longitudinal circulation—marked by the continuous window—are located on the southern facade.

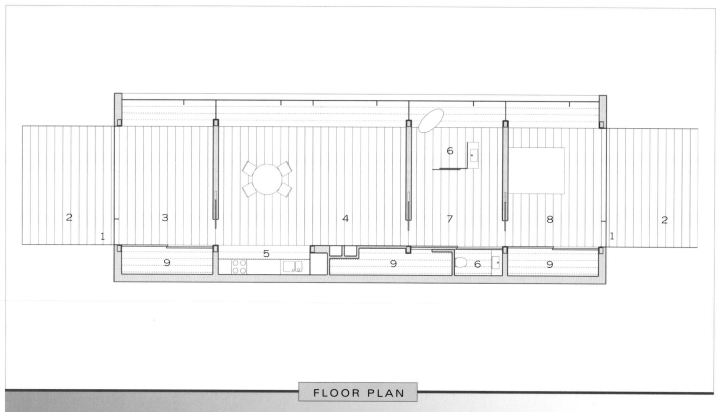

1. ENTRANCE
2. TERRACE
3. STUDY

4. LIVING / DINING AREA
5. KITCHEN
6. BATHROOM

7. BONSAI ROOM
8. BEDROOM
9. STORAGE / SERVICE

CROSS SECTION

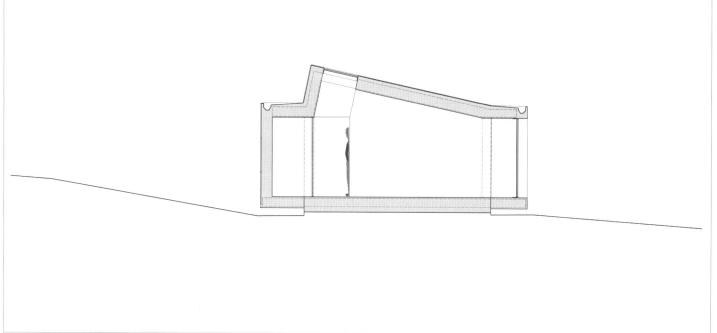

As far as construction is concerned, the house can be synthesized into "two parts—a slab of concrete paved with basalt and a shell of copper and glass."

The metallic structure is covered with a continuous exterior skin of copper panels that were manipulated in order to obtain a rugged texture.

"The slab was conceived of as a continual plane that runs from the terrace that receives the sunrise to the terrace that receives the sunset. Placed over this plane, the shell serves the functions of both facade and roof at the same time. It is closed off to the south, but open to the east, north, and west through a roof perforated by a continuous window that spatially separates the interior."

EVENING HILL HOUSE

Horden Cherry Lee Architects | Poole Harbour, Dorset, United Kingdom | PHOTOGRAPHER: DENNIS GILBERT (VIEW)

After long years of legal and bureaucratic conflict to obtain planning permission, the owners of this elegant house were able to build it. From its light anchorage on the land, it looks out onto the entrance to the harbor and onto Brownsea Island. This house is the culmination of more than thirty years of experience by Horden Cherry Lee Architects, beginning with the Courtyard House (1969). They follow the example of the Case Study Houses built in California in the 1950s—a project in which a series of determined models were superimposed and adapted to different places that all together constituted an experimental program in domestic architecture. Evening Hill House continues to explore the possibilities offered by glass and metal constructions, while reinterpreting them for this particular place

in which the house opens up to the south toward the views of the sea and, at the same time, toward the entrance patio situated to the north. The project contains a provision for a future extension of the house to the west, the direction in which it is to grow, as needed, in successive two-and-a-half-meter modules. In this way, a house is conceived that, taking advantage of the lay of the land, is laid out over two floors and will, while opening onto the landscape, achieve a state of "serene modernity."

The triangular plot, accessed from the northern facade, is inclined toward the south and looks out over the sea. This placement, in which the sun, the views, and the gradient are all oriented in the same southerly direction, leads to the house having

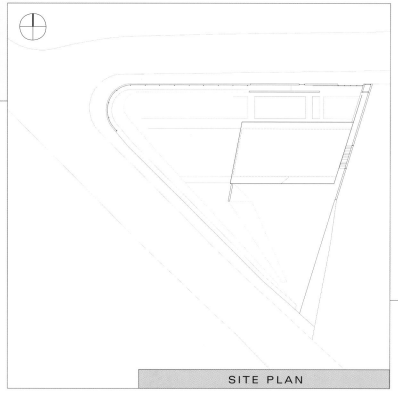

SITE PLAN

two levels. The upper level is situated over the entryway and is open to the landscape. The lower, partially buried area makes the most of the gradient and opens, on its southern face, to the views of the harbor entrance.

The access is reached by crossing a patio situated between the entrance wall and the volume of the house. Also situated on this upper floor are the garage, the kitchen, the study, and the living/dining room that looks out over the terrace to the sea. Below the access level, on the partially buried floor, the route to the bedrooms closely follows the exterior facade. This solution avoided the necessity of creating a passage in the dark part of the interior and allowed each bedroom to have its own bathroom.

The entire house has been conceived from the beginning on the principles of sustainability and energy efficiency that have consequently led to a diversity of solutions in the construction process. Among these, the use of the building's orientation toward the south to capture the solar radiation on the exterior paving and the walls of the lower floor stands out. This circumstance is avoided in summer, as the terrace has been designed as a regulatable light protector.

The solutions for energy efficiency are worth noting. These consist of the controlled solar-radiation absorption through the roof, which captures energy in summer and thermally insulates in winter, as well as the action of the white reflective screen on the patio, which balances the light levels in the living room and helps to reduce the energy losses in the northern face.

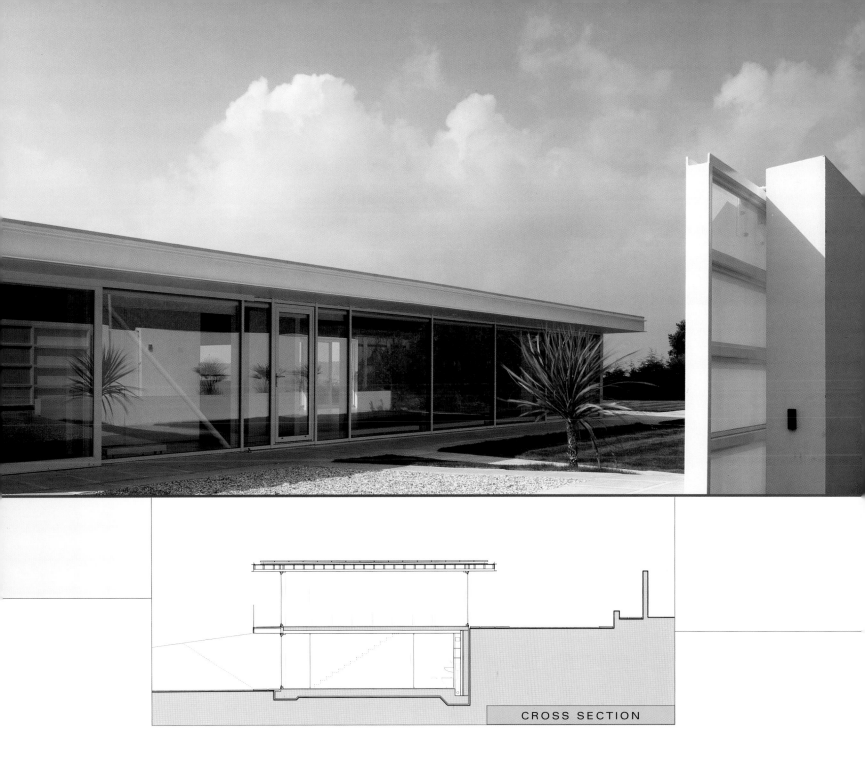

CROSS SECTION

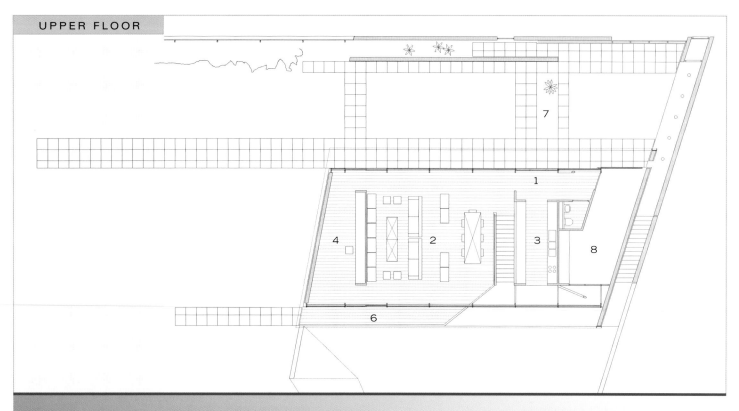

1. ENTRANCE
2. LIVING / DINING ROOM
3. KITCHEN

4. STUDY
5. BEDROOM
6. TERRACE

7. PATIO
8. GARAGE
9. STOREROOM / SERVICE

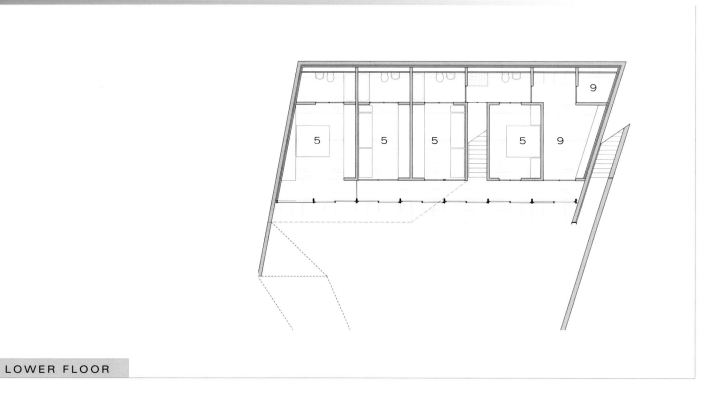

The division of the house on two levels is also manifested structurally since the steel-reinforced concrete retaining walls on the lower floor, which is underground with the exception of its southern face, are used as the foundations for the lightweight glass and steel architecture of the upper floor, which is completely open to the landscape.

CASA GOSTNNER

Studio Alberto Ponis | Costa Paradiso, Cerdeña, Italy | PHOTOGRAPHER: REINER BLUNCK

On a horizontal surface that covers the entire Costa Paradiso, in the northeast of the island of Sardinia, rises a lone strawberry tree, surrounded by evocative forms molded in granite over thousands of years. Based on the spatial and symbolic reference of this tree, situated among beautiful reddish rocks that dominate more than 180° of the Mediterranean Sea, Alberto Ponis built a hexagon that, through its apparently formal rigidity, has become a formidable yet compatible presence within the landscape.

It is a compact form, open to the views of the sea, that surrounds the strawberry tree while making the most of the rocks without touching them. It encloses a patio, an exterior space of shade and rest, protected from the sea winds.

The house, which is used as a second residence throughout the year, is distributed over two floors. On the upper floor, the hexagonal form contains in its central part—in contact with the patio and the terraces—the living room. The principal bedroom is situated in one of the extremes of the hexagon, while in another are located the kitchen and a guest room. On the lower floor, part of which has been excavated out of the underlying rock, the hexagon is broken in order to accommodate the cellar, two bedrooms, a gymnasium, and a sauna.

For a final touch, at a height intermediate to the house's floor levels, isolated among evocative rocky outcrops, a luminous swimming pool has been incorporated.

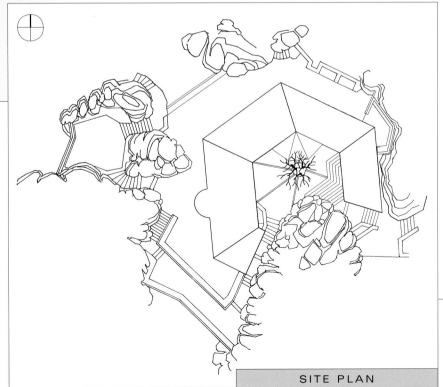

SITE PLAN

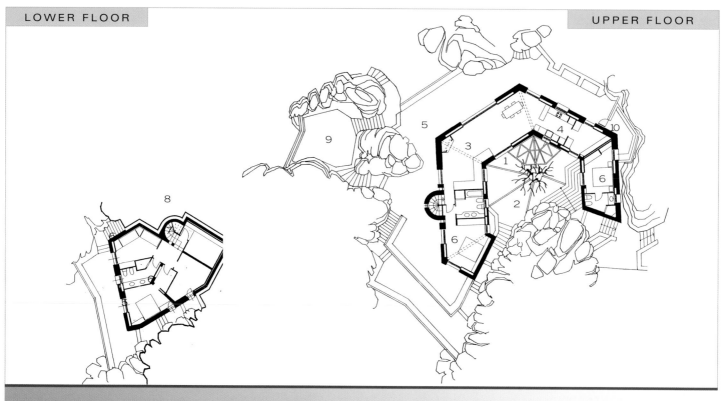

1. ENTRANCE
2. PATIO
3. LIVING / DINING AREA

4. KITCHEN
5. TERRACE
6. BEDROOM

7. GYM
8. CELLAR
9. SWIMMING POOL

10. STOREROOM /
SERVICE

The sloping tiled roof, the carpentry of the windows, and the omnipresent red granite support the delicate insertion of the house into the landscape and situate it within the architectural tradition of the area.

The interior spaces of the house radiate warmth thanks to the use of wood for the windows, doors, flooring, and in the infills between the beams as well as the beams themselves.

CROSS SECTION

Set in the rocks and surrounded by red granite, the swimming pool opens up to the immensity of the sea.

The exterior areas of the house are completely covered by stone, with the exception of the wooden paving around the swimming pool and on the upper terrace, the tinted concrete of the lintels, and the plaster of the patio walls, which have been finished in a red similar to the local stone.

Red granite was extracted from the plot and has been used in the paving, the steps, and the house's facades and retaining walls.

VILLA THOMKE

Julien Monfort architete | Port d'Alon, Côte d'Azur, France | PHOTOGRAPHERS: PHILIPPE RUAULT, JULIEN MONFORT

From a rocky outcrop in the middle of the inlet of Port d'Alon, a view of more than 220° of the Mediterranean Sea can be enjoyed. There, in the heart of the Côte d'Azur, on a plot with a gentle inclination toward the sea, stood a two-story stone and ceramic tiled house, which, as it was forty years old, the owner wished to refurbish. The refurbishing was meant to adapt the functionality of the house to present times and to modify its relationship to its exterior spaces. The intention was to improve the views of the sea, which, due to overgrown pine trees and a neighboring house, had become difficult to appreciate. The client also wanted to protect the exterior spaces of the house, on one hand, from the elements (the sun, rain, and strong mistral winds), and on the other, from the lack of privacy caused by the constant flow of bathers along a trail running beside

the house, which opened the old terraces to public display throughout the summer.

As a result of the client's requirements and the rigid but ambiguous urban regulations, Julien Monfort made a high-risk decision. He decided to extend the first floor of the house and cover it completely with a swimming pool to create a lookout from which the sea could be admired once again.

The preexisting house, in the form of an open "V," was extended toward the south, while the northern facade, which provides access, remained intact. The ground floor, where the bedrooms are located, was completely retained with the exception of the terrace, which was covered and protected from the wind. In contrast, the first floor was completely transformed and extended toward the south. The new

AERIAL VIEW OF THE SITE

VIEW OF THE PREEXISTING HOUSE

openings on this floor were conceived to give greater importance to the visual protection of the residence, with respect to the neighboring house as well as the bathers walking along the busy trail. To achieve this, the directions in which the views are enjoyed from the new spaces were carefully planned, a play on reflections and opacity was introduced into the windows, and, in the same way as on the ground floor, the "curves of shade" were used to protect not only from indiscreet exposure, but also from the weather.

The distribution of the rooms on the first floor follows the route of the sun: toward the east, the main bedrooms; toward the south, the living/kitchen area; and toward the west the "salon-library-fireplace-mini bar." The "niches," terraces, and bathrooms are situated among these three spaces. The roof is accessed by a staircase. From here, at a level higher than both the trees and the neighboring house, a splendid view of the horizon from east to west can be enjoyed, giving the sensation of being on an island surrounded by water. The wooden terracing is also used to conceal the machinery of the swimming pool, which, having a black bottom and the illusion that it overflows along its perimeter, creates the impression of being a continuation of the sea, interrupted only by its own limits, forming an artificial horizon.

ROOF FLOOR

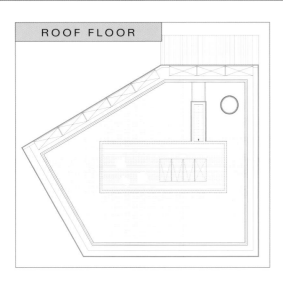

The favorable condition of the foundations and existing structural walls made the construction of the swimming pool feasible as it was only necessary to incorporate structural complements to support the great weight created by the change.

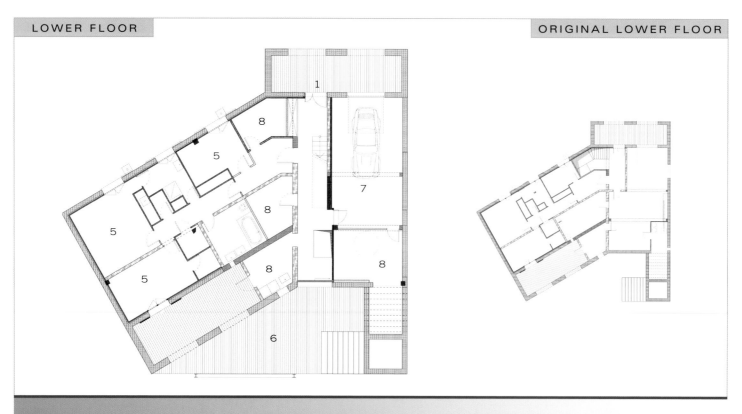

1. ENTRANCE
2. LIVING ROOM / KITCHEN
3. DINING ROOM
4. SALON / LIBRARY
5. BEDROOM
6. TERRACE
7. GARAGE
8. STOREROOM / SERVICE

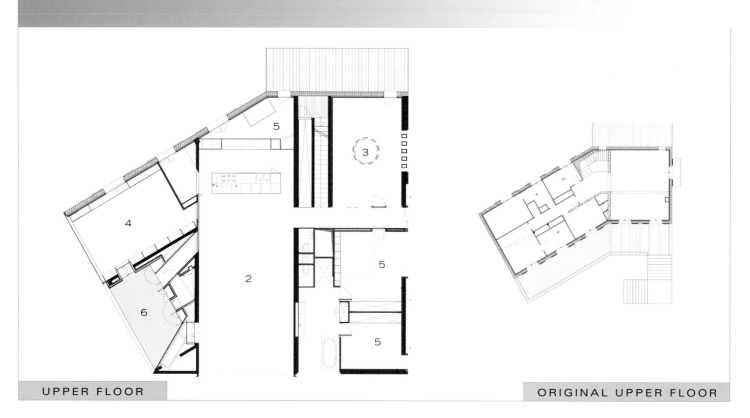

The new exterior walls were constructed in concrete tinted green to soften their impact on the landscape, while inside they are finished, as are the concrete floors, in gray. The windows are made of aluminum frames and various types of glass.

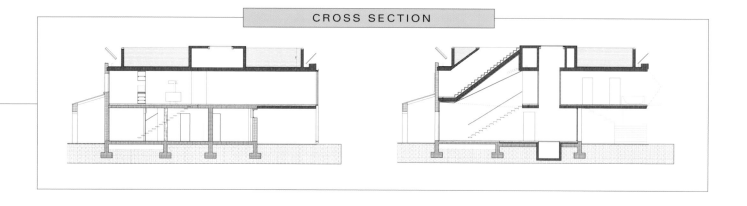

CROSS SECTION

In a search for a certain abstraction, the new materials were used to contrast with the original stone.

The swimming pool, surrounded by wooden floorboarding, was resolved in a mass of concrete faced with glass-reinforced polyester in a construction solution intended to protect the house from the dangers of humidity.

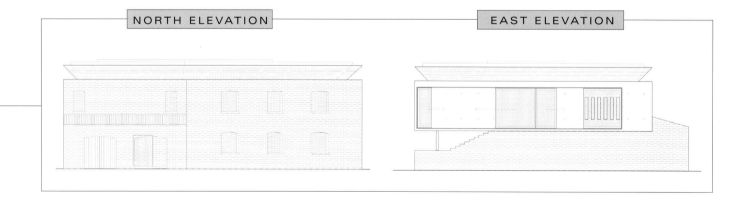

NORTH ELEVATION

EAST ELEVATION

An intervention that contrasts the new with the preexisting has been established while respecting the old and "using" the old architecturally, but not overpowering it.

CASA
NA XAMENA

Ramón Esteve | Na Xamena, Ibiza, Spain | PHOTOGRAPHER: RAMÓN ESTEVE

Na Xamena was discovered during the search for a place in which to site a house; or, perhaps, it was Na Xamena itself that decided where the house should be constructed. And in the solitude surrounding the rocks and junipers, with a horizon determined by cliffs that fade away and enter into the light of the Mediterranean Sea, this place in the northeast of the island of Ibiza is a timeless space. "After so many centuries of changeless landscape," the site demanded from Ramón Esteve a reverent attitude toward a project that respected the equilibrium of the place, its surroundings, and culture. "From the initial phases of the project, as much in the choice of materials and colors as in the organization of volumes and establish-

ing the form of construction, although everything was developed from a rational base that reinforced the unity of the whole, it was defined without being limited to a rigid geometric scheme." The house, built in three phases, was conceived as a continual growing organism dictated by the guidelines of its original nucleus. The addition of the differing cubic bodies, reminiscent of the traditional architecture of Ibiza, complies with the idea of a sequence of spaces with measurements that vary proportionally in their three dimensions and that trace an ordered route of growth while ascending from the rocky base.

The house is defined as being "all compact and of apparent simplicity that establishes a parallel with the morphology of the cliffs"

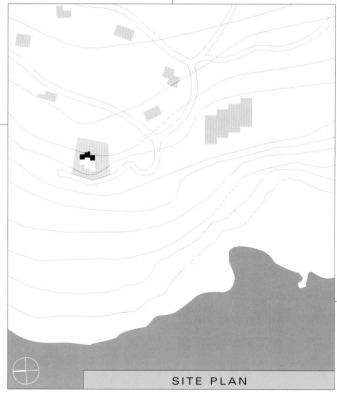

SITE PLAN

and that orders, by means of the levels of the terraces, the swimming pool, crowned by the rounded geometry of its volumes. It's an intervention that harmonizes with its surroundings in a logical sequence of land and landscape.

Within the play on volumes, the entrance is situated on the upper floor. On this floor, the main spaces of the house have been concentrated—the kitchen, living room, and dining room—along with the two principal bedrooms with their respective services, while the studio has been situated on a mezzanine (over the landing and facing the living room). Independent of these spaces, on a lower level that takes advantage of the unevenness of the land, a

bedroom is situated on the north face and another two, beside the garage, in the southern part of the house. The different levels on which the floors were planned make the space more dynamic and define the exterior areas—such as the terrace and the swimming pool—that possess their own entity and that are oriented toward the landscape, allowing the Mediterranean Sea to be enjoyed at any time of the day. All of the exterior spaces were completed with the geometry of the steps that provide access to the house and terraces and give shape to this area, which was extracted from the land and is enclosed by water and benches made from old wooden railway sleepers.

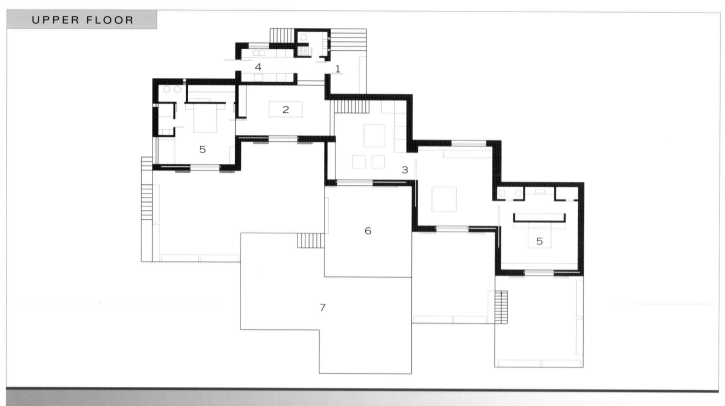

1. ENTRANCE
2. DINING ROOM
3. LIVING ROOM
4. KITCHEN
5. BEDROOM
6. TERRACES
7. SWIMMING POOL
8. GARAGE

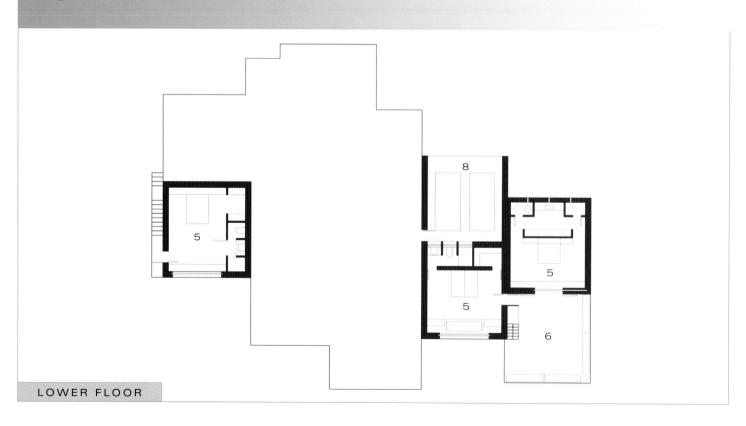

Alongside the white of the walls, with lines in cobalt blue, and the gray of the floors, iroko wood was used for the rest of the interior finishes: in the wooden planking that runs from the living room to the roof and the walls of the dining room, in the studio staircase, around the sunken bathtub to the interior doors lacquered in white, or even hidden in the partition walls. It has also been used in the carpentry of the windows that are embedded in the walls to strengthen the overall effect of the house.

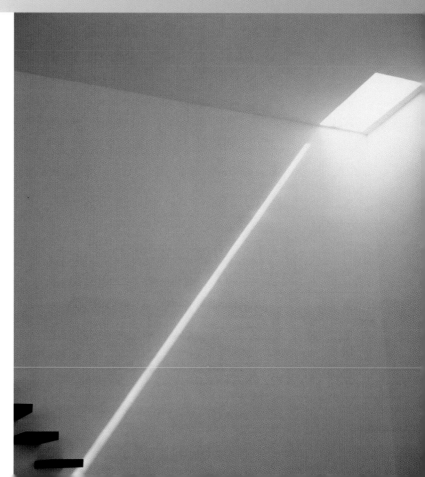

The exterior walls, clean and naked, are perforated according to the interior arrangements, which leads to the predominance of the forms over the voids. White has been used in the vertical planes and gray in the concrete paving in a color scheme that helps unify the masses of the added volumes.

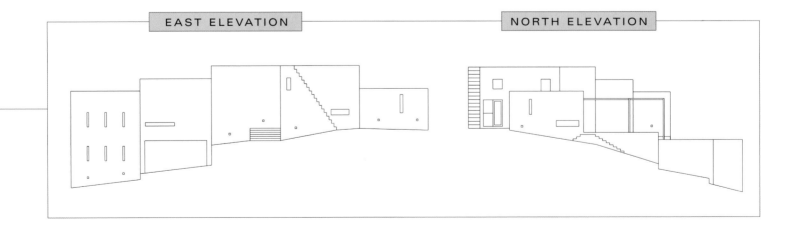

EAST ELEVATION

NORTH ELEVATION

The house, through the sequence of spaces that have been opened from the inside to the outside, aims to create a form of timeless architecture that synthesizes all of the qualities of a fragile and marvelous place.

CASA TORRES

A-Cero arquitectura y urbanismo | A Coruña, Galicia, Spain | PHOTOGRAPHERS: ÁNGEL BALTANÁS, XURXO LOBATO

A triangular plot is surrounded by a complex built-up area sloping downward to meet, on its northern side, a precipice that looks out over the estuary of A Coruña. This is one of many geographical points on the Galician coast where the Atlantic Ocean penetrates deeply inland to create natural enclaves of breathtaking beauty in which seawater mixes with the freshwater from the numerous small rivers that find their way through the undulating Galician topography.

To harmonize with the place and to complement the topological inclination and visual orientation, A-Cero designed a house inclined toward the estuary; a house in which two connected volumes serve the interior and exterior spaces in a search for a "materialization directly related to the sculptural activity of eliminating material from a compact volume."

Through volumetric severity, the facade is accentuated to deal cleanly with the empty spaces in a house that seeks, through purity of form and space, a scale relating as much to its immediate setting, in which a preexisting centennial chestnut tree has determined the layout of the different elements of the house, as to its more distant surroundings, since the house forms part of one of the elevated areas of the city that is clearly seen when entering A Coruña.

"The residence, in this way, is clearly open to the mouth of the estuary and radically closed on the side that borders the access road."

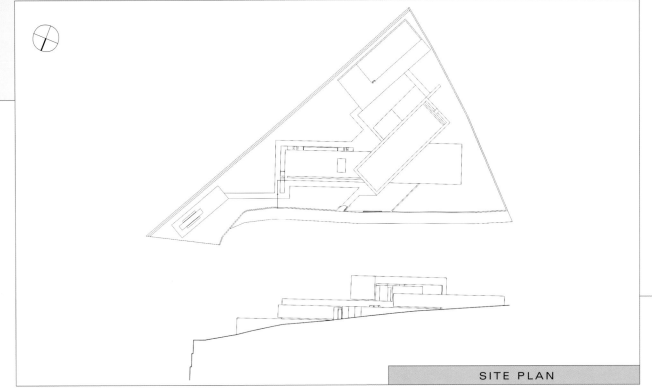

SITE PLAN

Situated on the intersection of the axes of the two volumes that make up the house, the main staircase constitutes the functional distributor of each of the three floors. In the basement, this axis of vertical circulation provides access to the office and the projection room while the guest rooms are situated on an intermediate level. Rising up to the floor on which the access is situated, the staircase separates the kitchen from the living room and from the garage, while on the upper floor, oriented toward the double-sized living/dining area, it gives access to the owners' bedroom. This bedroom is unique because of its size, which makes it a third independent piece completely disconnected from the axis and also from the volume in which it is situated.

The house is intended to discover "new perspectives of every-day life directly related to Galician culture," such as giving spatial and functional importance to the kitchen or the use of autochthonous materials—slate used as much on the roof and facade—in an attempt to establish the concept of a family residence while giving equal value to different scales: urban, architectural, and detail.

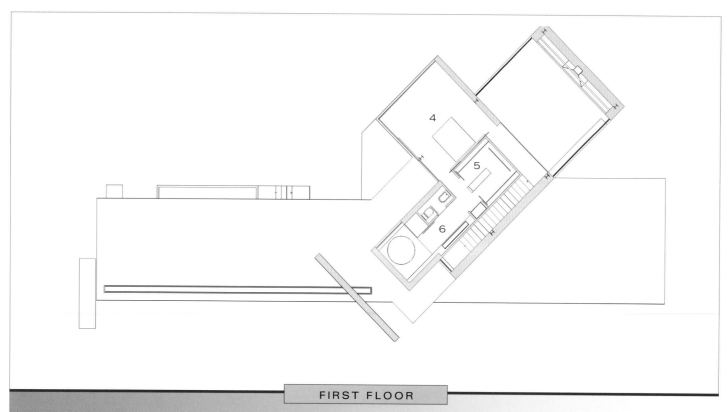

FIRST FLOOR

1. ENTRANCE
2. LIVING / DINING AREA
3. KITCHEN
4. BEDROOM
5. DRESSING ROOM
6. BATHROOM
7. GARAGE
8. STOREROOM / SERVICE

GROUND FLOOR

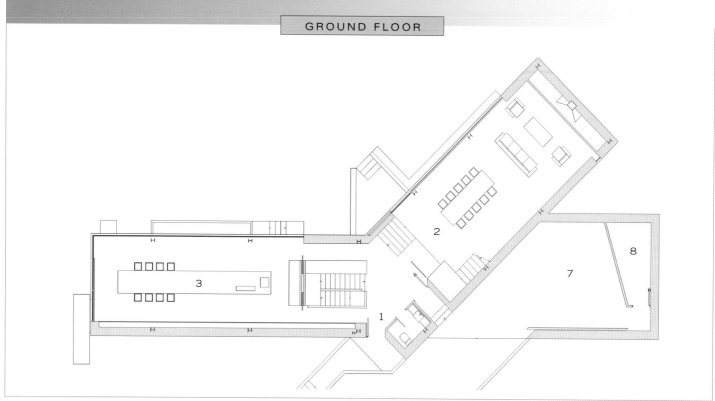

The building solutions adopted reflect the search for dynamism, spatial richness, and purity of volume desired for the project. Examples of this intention in the construction are the elimination of all elements that could distract from a direct perception of the spaces (skirting boards, joint covers, and so on...) and in the way in which the interior is unified chromatically: the floors, walls, and ceilings have all been painted white.

The structural elements were designed to the perimeter of the volumes, leaving the interior spaces clear of any structural obligations.

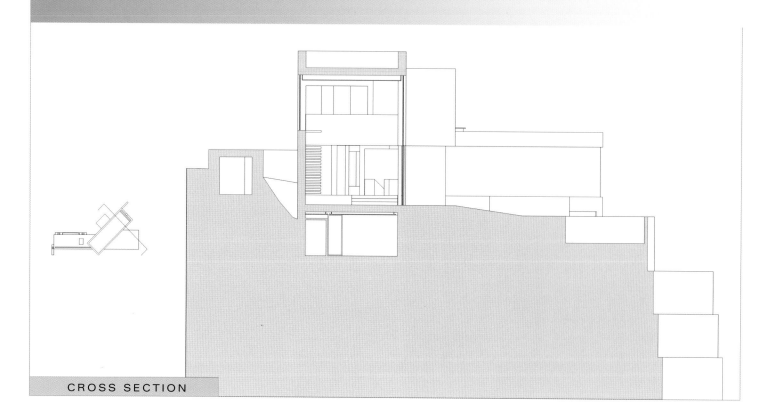

CROSS SECTION

The facades and principal volumes, which are entirely covered in slate, tend to transfer formal and spatial purity onto the details of the construction as a whole.

CASA EM OFIR

José Fernando Gonçalves, Cristina Guedes | Ofir, Porto, Portugal | PHOTOGRAPHERS: ALESSANDRA CHEMOLLO, JOSÉ F. GONÇALVES

The Green Coast is a region of Northwest Portugal which, due to the high level of rainfall that it receives, has abundant vegetation on its undulating landscape, which gently slopes down toward the Atlantic Ocean. In this territory, there are beautiful sandy beaches that foster small, quaint villages, some of which are going through major transformations due to strong urban pressure typical of many coastal areas around the world. Ofir is one of these attractive places in which the contemporary urban culture induces development based only on economic parameters, overlookng the fact that architecture was (until the twentieth century) a complex instrument used to create harmonious relationships between man and his surroundings. While present-day societies seem to be unable to come to terms with this serious urban problem, both the client and the architects, José F. Gonçalves and Cristina Guedes, sought the best possible solution and designed a house that would be an example of the harmony that should exist between place and architecture.

Surrounded by a mass of family residences set, with relative discretion, behind a large sandy beach, this house sensitively responds to the challenge of constructing on the virgin dunes of a fragile ecosystem. A building that "respects nature and the topographical characteristics of the land," it takes advantage of the gentle incline of the site to bury the major part of its volume. The resulting house, in which the play of the glazed planes with the local stone, volumes, and

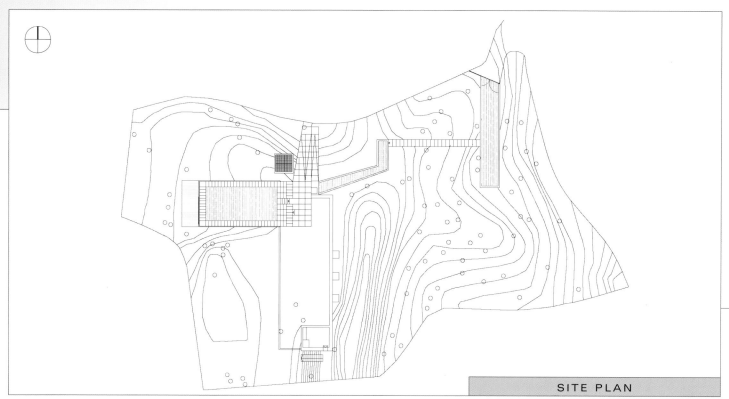

SITE PLAN

roofs leaves the exterior spaces in their wild state, is an achievement in the sought-for integration of the house with its setting.

This shelter/house has been laid out over various levels in its adaptation to the lay of the land and arranged in the form of an "L" that separates it into two parts from a functional point of view. The long side of the floor plan, practically buried in the sand and trimmed with a flat, gardened roof, accommodates the access. To the right, open to a patio, are the installations, while to the left, along the length of the "L," are a game room and three bedrooms—with their respective bathrooms—which are open to the access facade. At the other end of the house, opening to the patio, are the principal bedroom and a bathroom. Situated on a higher level is the short arm of the "L," which is accessed by a staircase that starts in the hall and reaches the only stepped space in the building. Here we find the kitchen, dining room, and living room. This space has been finished off with an inclined roof that follows the contours of the land, and in which the interior spaces are totally open to the dunes and the sea through the large glassed areas.

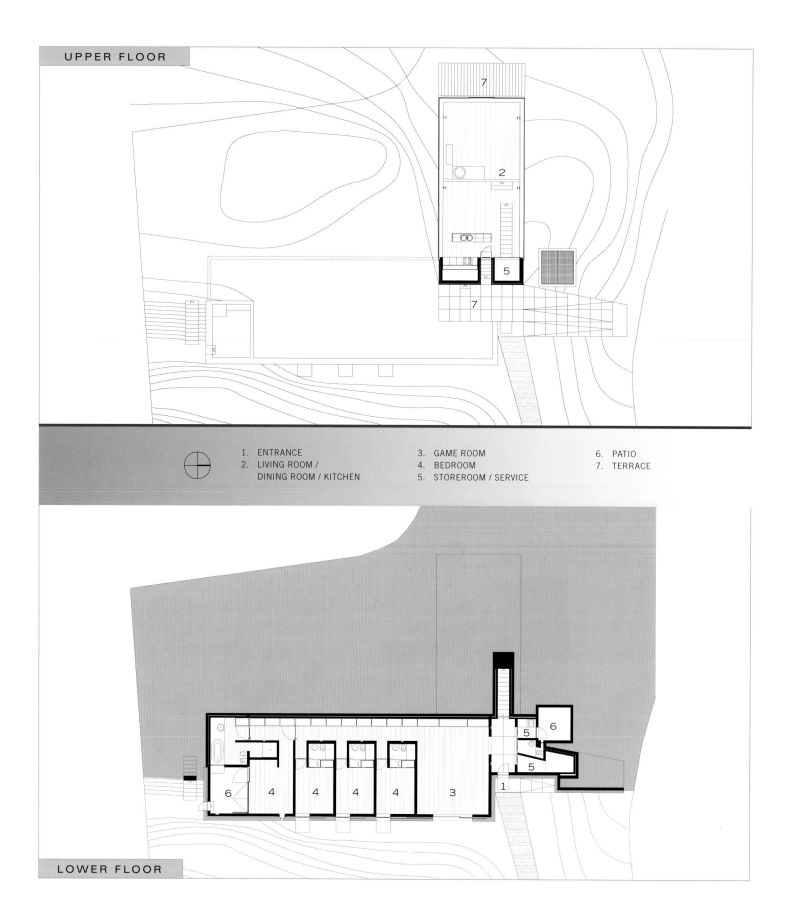

UPPER FLOOR

1. ENTRANCE
2. LIVING ROOM /
   DINING ROOM / KITCHEN
3. GAME ROOM
4. BEDROOM
5. STOREROOM / SERVICE
6. PATIO
7. TERRACE

LOWER FLOOR

To "preserve the natural characteristics of the vegetation, only the strictly necessary exterior surfaces were paved." These are the parking areas, the access drive to the house, and the ramp that takes us up onto the inclined roof, which was also paved in local stone.

In the interior spaces, the cold gray of the concrete, which is also present in all of the partition walls of the bedrooms, contrasts with the warmth of the wood used in the flooring, doors, and wardrobes, leaving the bathrooms as an exception, as they have been finished in marble.

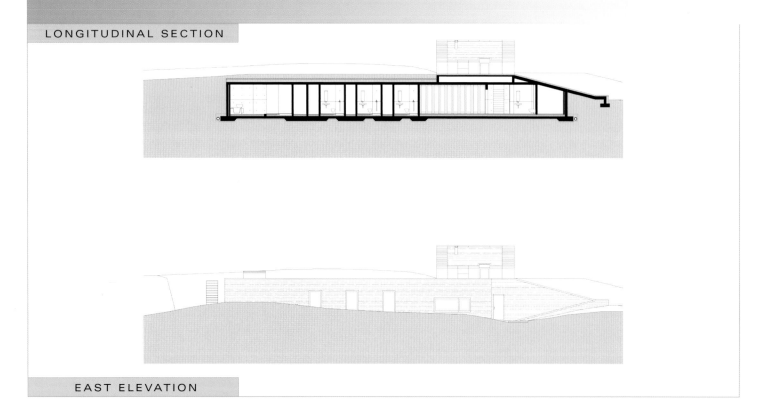

LONGITUDINAL SECTION

EAST ELEVATION

In order to obtain optimum insulation from the humidity of the land, the walls were constructed as double walls with a cavity and were faced with local stone, while their interiors are steel-reinforced concrete constructed in situ. These serve as structural elements as well as providing the interior finishes. In the living room space, the structure is based on metal pillars that support the slab of reinforced concrete with which all of the roofs have been built.

MAINE DWELLING

Peter Forbes | Great Cranberry Island, Maine, United States

The house rises over a special site in which open meadow, forest, and the sea all come together. Halfway between the large glazed surfaces of coastal residences and the wooden structure of a mountain refuge, the house becomes a tool that unifies everything in its surroundings. In a context marked by a strong dual component, as far as landscape is concerned, the house offers two facades with two completely different views.

The project was based on the use of two very long single-story pavilions set quite close to each other at an obtuse angle. They are intentionally geometrically simple so as to center all of our senses on the beauty of the location. The segregation allows the owners' living areas to be situated on one side and those destined for guests on the other. At the closest point between the two volumes, two large chimney stacks in stone come together to form something of a portico, which acts as a filter between the forest of conifers and the ocean and constitutes the access to the house across an intermediate courtyard.

The larger body is situated horizontally across another, smaller volume and marks the separation between the relaxation area and the more private area. The result of the three volumes, which are separate but tightly linked, is a succession of spaces that flow into one another thanks to the large openings in the panels that separate the various environments.

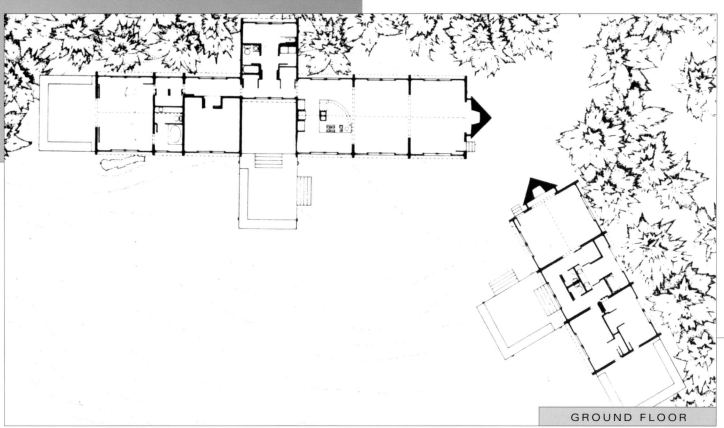

The house rises on wooden posts that help to keep humidity away from the floor while also solving the problems presented by building over an irregular rocky terrain.

Moving from one end to the other, we come across the living room with fireplace, the dining room, and the kitchen as well as a study and the bedrooms, with their corresponding bathrooms on the opposite side. In turn, the guests' area includes bedrooms, living/dining room, and kitchen. Both blocks have the benefit of a centrally located lookout terrace designed as a place from which views of the sea can be enjoyed. Structurally, the residence has been laid out following a series of cross walls that hold up a pitched roof. The facades contain numerous openings of different sizes: large sliding glass panels on the longitudinal aspect and smaller windows on the lateral. In this way, a large amount of natural light reaches all corners of the residence. As much in the interior as in the exterior, the surfaces are in a wide variety of woods, ranging from cedar to mahogany and spruce.

SECTION

LONG ISLAND DWELLING

Steven Haas | Long Island, New York, United States

This house, located on the Atlantic coast of the United States, rises on a rectangular floor plan and adopts a play on its glazed curvilinear walls to form part of an overall dynamic composition as an authentic reflection of the view that can be enjoyed from within. The front entrance to the building is maintained as the most private part of the house, and it is here that the outdoor games area can be found, with croquet and badminton courts and a two-hundred-year-old beech tree as a backdrop. The distribution of the house over two levels allows for the private living areas upstairs to be separate from the public entertainment areas on the ground floor. The main entrance is found at the back of the house through an approach created alongside a good-sized garage that can accommodate a number of vehicles. Once inside and heading off the hall to the left, we reach the service area and auxiliary spaces. In the center of the house, facing south, we find the principal area of the project: the large living room, the dining room—and the kitchen, separated from the rest by a counter. Beyond this area, there is a study/library that is perfectly isolated by means of solid walls.

Upstairs, the master bedroom, complete with dressing room and bathroom, opens onto a large uncovered terrace. Two simple bedrooms open onto the other open-air space and, in front, the space is completed with the children's playroom. The connection between the two levels is resolved by a staircase leading from the main living area, accompanied by a series of hollows in the ceiling that allow light to

DETAIL OF THE TEAK WALKWAYS

flow through. Having started with a limited surface area and a resi-dential context in which the units were too close to each other, the architect tried to catch the fabulous views of the sea and escape from the nearby constructions. This led to the incorporation of the large glazed facade that looks out onto the ocean and solid side walls in granite and bands of slate. The 7,000-square-foot construction was designed with the strong north winds in mind. The architect made use of available technologies to cater to such circumstances. The project is characterized by the way in which it maintains the major-ity of its spaces in direct contact with the outside by means of its glass floor-to-roof wall.

The light and the landscape are integrated in the interior through the large glazed surfaces of the facade. On the exterior, between the house and the water, dikes, terraces, plantings, and the beach are all connected by a series of teak planks that invite a stroll.

The house is situated facing the sea and is separated from it by no more than a dynamic glass wall, which is completely transparent and which reflects the sweeping waves of water as they reach the coast.

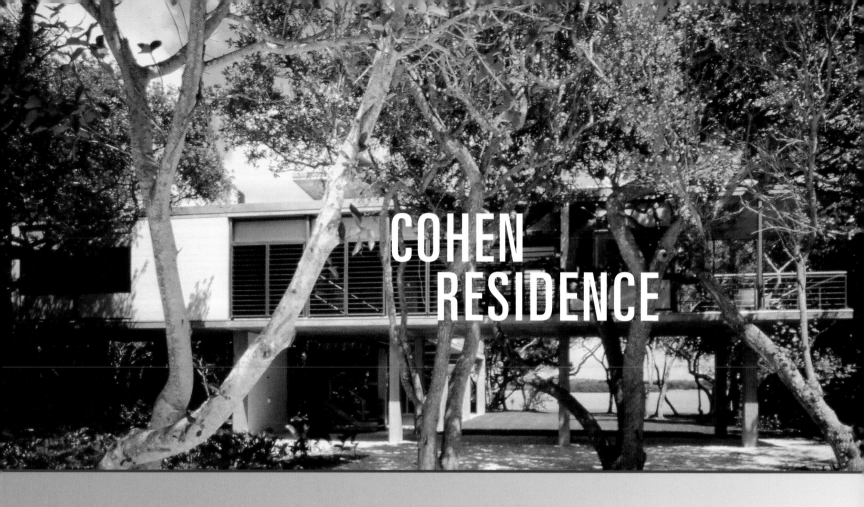

COHEN RESIDENCE

Toshiko Mori Architects | Sarasota, Florida, USA | PHOTOGRAPHER: PAUL WORCHOL

The Florida Keys is a series of narrow, lushly green sand tongues, that lies lie off the coast and constitutes an exceptional ecosystem where only a few of the privileged are able to own a house. In Cayo Key, the owners of a house designed by the architect Paul Rudolph in the 1950s wanted to extend their residence by constructing an independent pavilion for their children. This was to be built on the same plot, situated on a sandy strip 160 meters wide that separates two protected reserves, one dedicated to the turtles of the Mexican Coast and the other to the manatees of Sarasota Bay. In this exceptional place, Toshiko Mori constructed a pavilion over the ruins of an area that was swept away by one of the hurricanes that periodically devastate this area. This conditioning climatic aspect, along with the high degree of solar radiation, the strong storms, and frequent flooding, led to the decision of raising the house five meters

above the level of the sea. Thus, the new section does not obstruct the views of either coastline, as it is situated in the treetops of the mangoes, oaks, and palms that still surround the house. "The construction responds to the intensity of the climate, as its inhabitable area has been raised on pillars that are higher than the crest of a wave. It also responds to the dense vegetation by which it is surrounded and that it uses to obtain both shade and privacy."

Conceived as a tribute to the "Sarasota School," of which the architect Paul Rudolph was a member, the residence has a floor plan in the form of a "T," is aligned along the principal axis of the existing house, and shares the same need to respond to the hot and humid climate through its design elements. It reinterprets the styles of the traditional houses of the area, which make the most of the movements of air from one area to another. A narrow form has been cre-

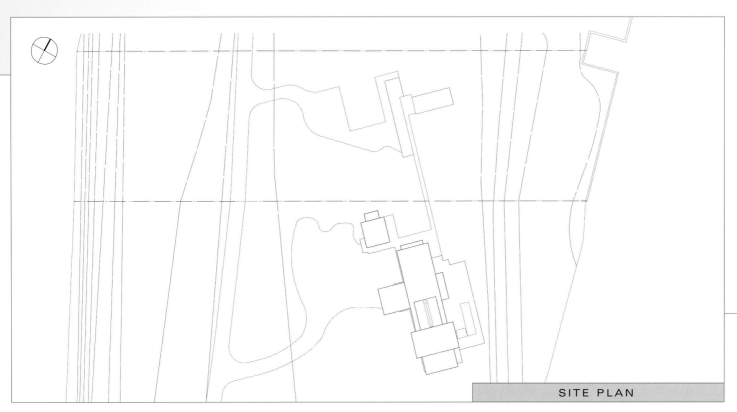

SITE PLAN

ated and raised among the trees, constructed with "minimal details and elementary materials" that enable it to adapt to the location in a rational and sensitive way.

The new house, dedicated to the clients' three children, consists of two forms that are articulated around an exterior staircase and make up a floor plan in the form of a "T." The stairs guarantee the functional unity of the whole, as well as the independence of the two structures that, raised on pillars over the site, are perceived as one volume. The longest and narrowest wing of the extension is aligned on the axis of the hosue designed by Paul Rudolph and accommo-

dates, on one floor, the common areas of the residence—living/dining area and kitchen—next to one of the three bedrooms. The other two bedrooms, with their respective bathrooms and living rooms, are situated on each of the two floors' perpendicular bodies.

All of the floors make the most of their elevated position and are open to the views of Sarasota Bay. A terrace for each floor has been established, one next to the kitchen in the extreme south of the common space and the other on the second floor of the orthogonal form.

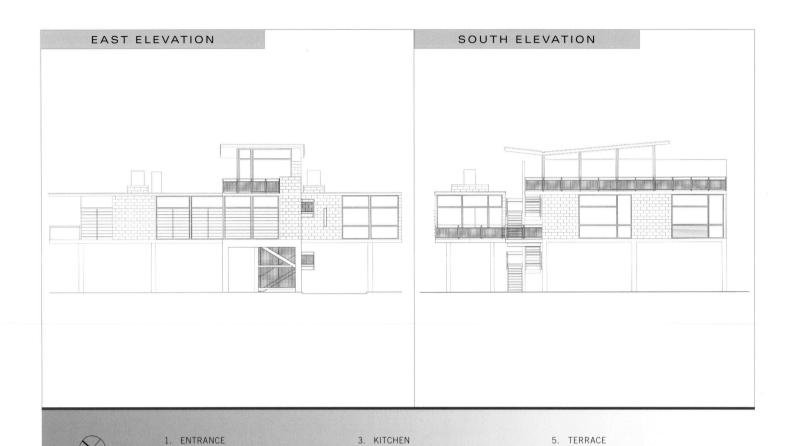

EAST ELEVATION

SOUTH ELEVATION

1. ENTRANCE
2. LIVING / DINING ROOM
3. KITCHEN
4. BEDROOM
5. TERRACE
6. GARDEN

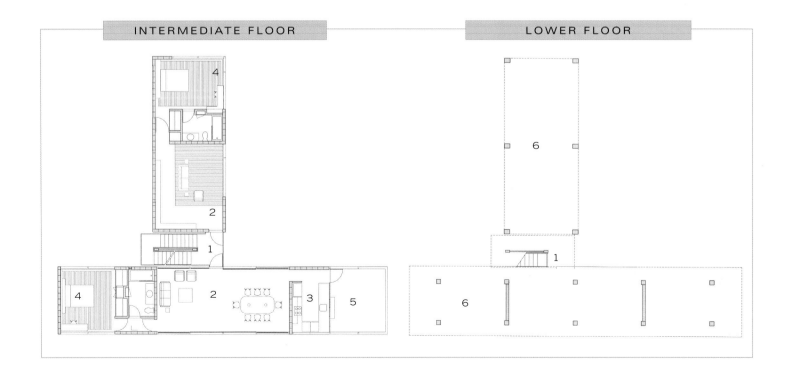

INTERMEDIATE FLOOR

LOWER FLOOR

Along with the concrete and metal of the structure, in the facade of the building, there is a block of bare concrete that is used as much as a finish for the facades as for its structural capacity. Glass in transparent, translucent, and etched finishes is mounted in steel frames, and metal plates are arranged around the openings to offer protection from the sun.

The structure of the building, with its foundations sunk more than six meters below sea level, has been calculated to support extreme weather conditions. It is based on a mixed structure of steel-reinforced concrete, used in the lower pillars and in the slabs of the infills, and metal, which is only present in the pillars on the second floor.

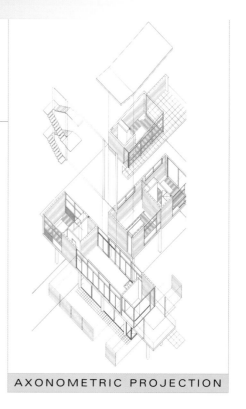

AXONOMETRIC PROJECTION

The different materials make up facades with "difference in opacity that give life and variety to the building that would otherwise appear as a hermetic glass box." They also establish a neutral tone for the new construction that finds itself surrounded by an exceptional array of colors ranging from the green of the vegetation to the intense blues of the sea. This, again, shows the discretion that was applied to the house.

LAKE ERIE HOUSE

EFM Design | Lake Erie, Ontario, Canada | PHOTOGRAPHERS: DAVID WHITTAKER, EMANUELA FRATTINI

Thousands of years ago, the thawing of large glaciers in North America created five freshwater seas known as the Great Lakes that, while cutting through the United States and Canada, constitute the largest freshwater system in the world. Beginning in Lake Superior, it descends along Saint Mary's River to Lake Michigan and Lake Huron, then flows down the Detroit River to reach Lake Erie. The water continues its search for the sea and runs along the Niagara River, over the famous Niagara Falls, into Lake Ontario and along the Saint Lawrence River, to finally reach the Atlantic Ocean, the destination of its magnificent course of more than 3,700 kilometers.

On the shores of Lake Erie, in the Canadian province of Ontario, a couple whose main residence is in Buffalo, New York, wished to build a second home on a large plot of land that ran down, on its southern side, to meet the shores of Lake Erie. The New York office of EFM Design constructed a house based on the idea of maximizing the views of the lake despite the limitations imposed by the geometry of the plot. As a result, three articulated volumes have been arranged around a patio with the intention of visually "maintaining and respecting the spirit of a traditional Ontario home, as much in its interior spaces as in its external appearance." The result is based on ideas of simplicity and warmth, in a location that, while overlooking the lake, offers protection during the long months of low temperatures and opens up to the outside when the warm summer arrives.

Three sections of the house, which was conceived as a second residence for a couple without children, have been laid out around an enclosed patio and have been sited on the long and narrow plot

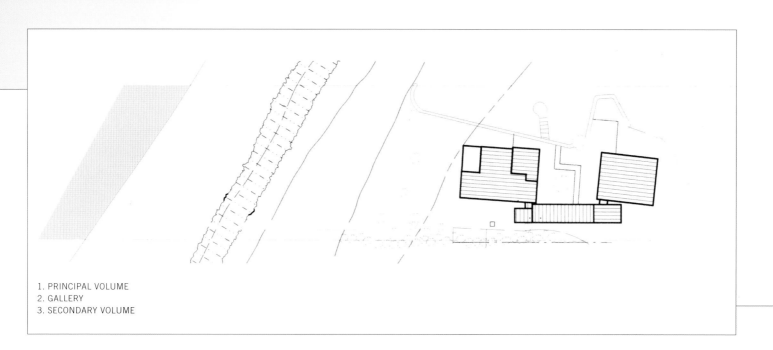

1. PRINCIPAL VOLUME
2. GALLERY
3. SECONDARY VOLUME

that overlooks the lake from its shortest side. The part closest to the lake contains the nucleus of the clients' home and touches, with one of its highest points at the back, the second part, which, in the form of a gallery, serves to join the principal section with the part that serves as a guest residence. All three open onto the patio and are arranged so that views of the lake can be enjoyed from the upper floor of the guest section.

The visitors' access leads directly to the principal volume across the patio, while the service entrance is through the garage, situated on the ground floor of the posterior two-floor volume. On the upper floor is the guest residence, consisting of a living room, two bed-

rooms, a terrace, and a bathroom. The staircase to this floor is situated in the gallery and is mainly used (apart from a storage place and for services) to connect the principal volume. On the lower floor of the lakeside volume is the living/dining room, and in the back area, beside the patio, are the kitchen and a lavatory. A staircase leads from the living room area to the upper floor, where there is the bedroom, a library that looks onto the living room through a double space, a gym, a bathroom, and a terrace. Up on another floor, a studio-lookout area, which constitutes another element of the attractive compositional play of the house, juts out over the principal volume.

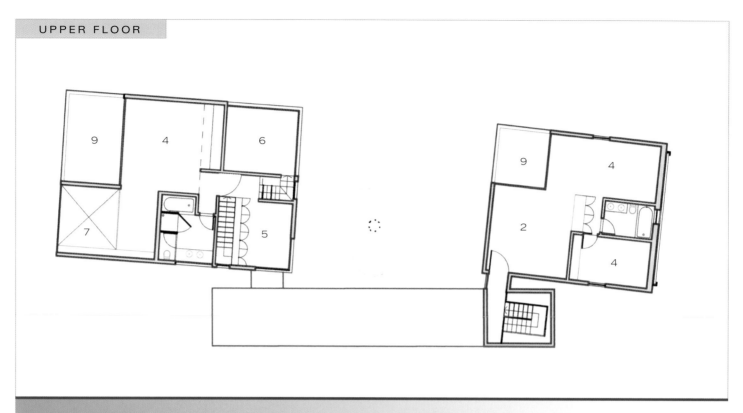

1. ENTRANCE	4. BEDROOM	7. HOLLOW	10. GARAGE
2. LIVING / DINING ROOM	5. GYM	8. PATIO	11. SERVICE
3. KITCHEN	6. STUDY	9. TERRACE	

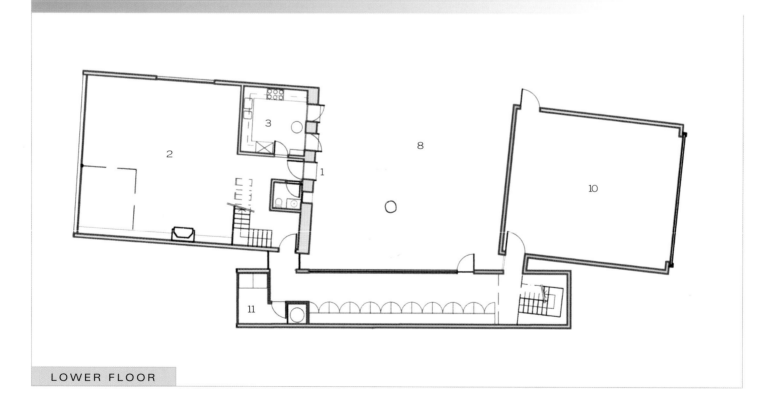

The zinc panels (also used for roofing), cedar, and masonry in local stone form facades that contrast to and relate with each other.

The warm interiors have been achieved by using, along with the white of the walls and ceilings, local materials such as cedar and dark-colored stone that is used for the kitchen flooring and gallery.

WEST ELEVATION

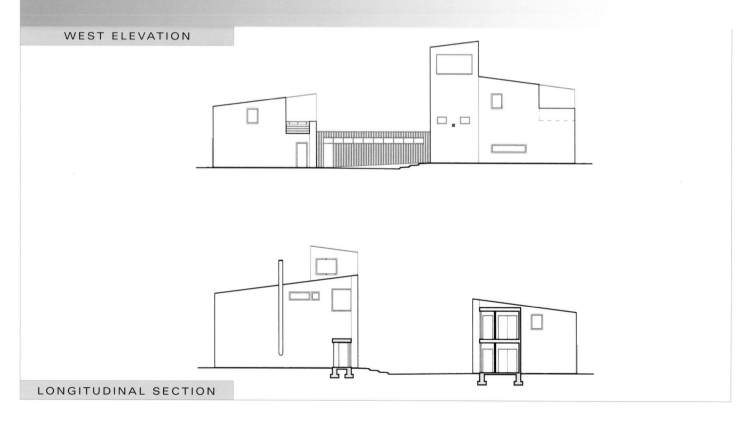

LONGITUDINAL SECTION

The entire house is an attractive play of volumes complemented by their different finishes.

MALIBU HOUSE

Richard Meier & Partners | Malibu, California, United States

This Malibu Beach house is sited on a flat terrain, made up originally of three separate plots. The two-floor residence is in an "L" form. The areas for entertaining are on the ground floor and the private areas are on the upper level. On the protected north side, the main entrance leads to a fully glazed double-height hall. From this space, the large living room, the dining room, the kitchen and service area, and the guest rooms are accessed. The stairs that originate in the open space of the living room lead to the second floor, on which there are various rooms as well as the master bedroom with its own dressing room and bathroom. The spatial succession of the compo-sition is complemented by a preexisting tennis court in the southern zone and a new swimming pool in the eastern zone. The principal objective of the project was to achieve a high level of connection between interior and exterior, establishing a direct link between the house and the views of the sea. For this reason, there is an interior courtyard as an extension of the living room, which allows the climate of the area to be enjoyed. In fact, large windows make up the greater part of the wall surfaces to reinforce the spirit of spatial fusion sought by the architect. More specifically, this can be seen in the materials and finishes that are repeated inside and outside.

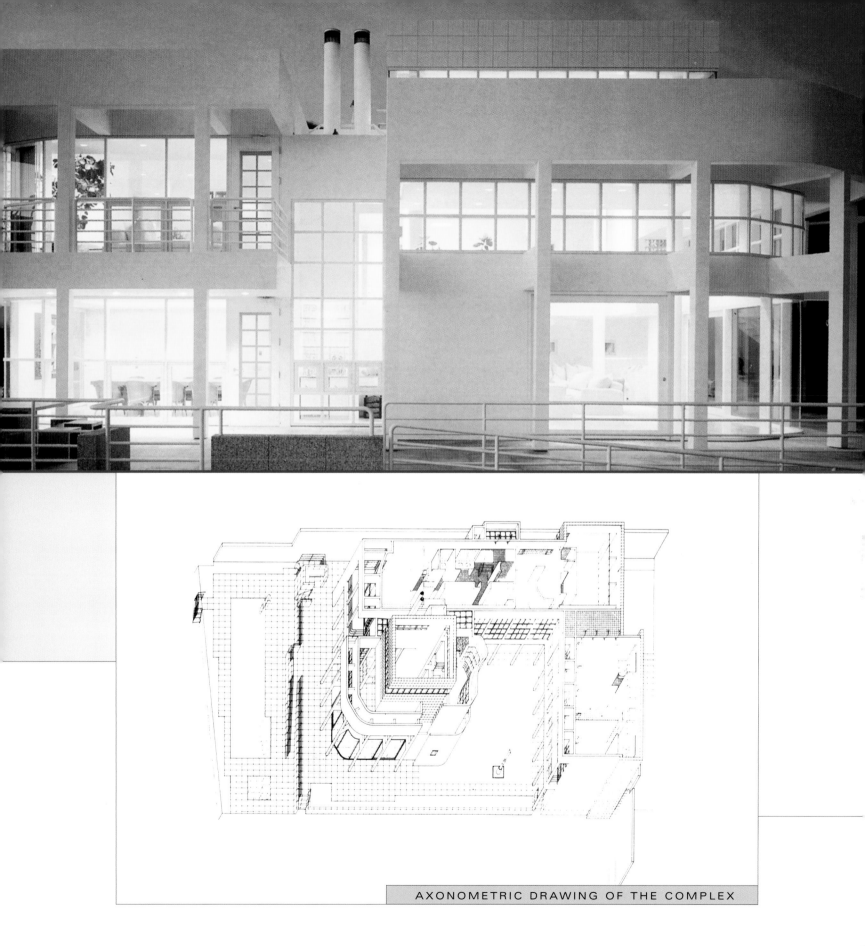

AXONOMETRIC DRAWING OF THE COMPLEX

At night, the large windows and the illumination achieve almost complete transparency with the surroundings. During the day, this is achieved by means of the hedge in the garden and is also present in the contrasting blue water of the swimming pool and the marine horizon. Throughout, columns, used rectilinearly or in curves, constitute one of the features that characterize this construction from every perspective. In addition, the white of the walls and ceilings becomes an outstanding feature as much on the inside as on the outside of the house. A system of latticework and skylights modulates and controls the changing California light and the excesses of sun and heat, while also achieving an interesting play of shadows and reflections. In counterpoint to the rectilinear geometric forms of the complex, an undulating wall is found in the living room, opening onto the interior garden and producing an effect of movement.

The white color and the large windows come together in an exercise of composition and contribute to the interaction between the interior and the exterior by means of the same materials, colors, and textures used in all of the areas.

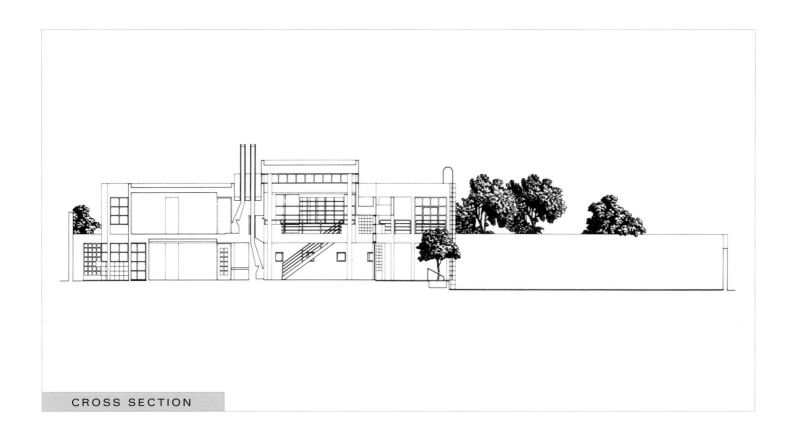

CROSS SECTION

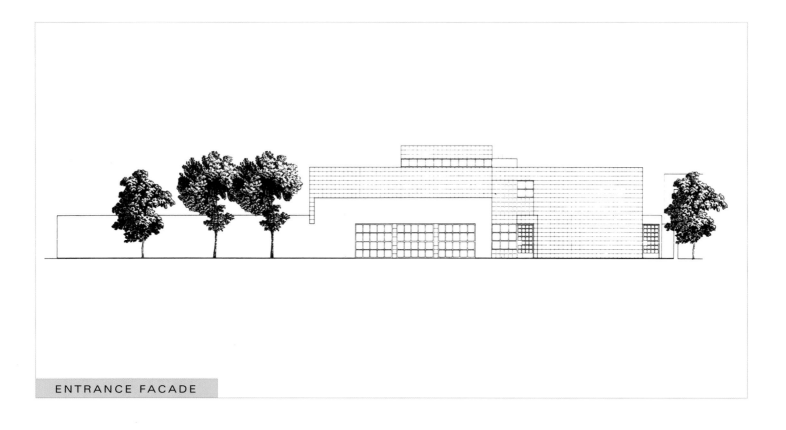

ENTRANCE FACADE

The skillful use of white, which fills every corner and element of the house, captures and reflects the particular light conditions of the house's placement by the sea.

In the interior, the spaces flow from one to another and enjoy the different illumination that enters through the windows and skylights. The tones and textures of the furniture are in harmony with the unified character of the composition that reserves the use of color and contrasts for the decorative elements.

CAPISTRANO BEACH HOUSE

Rob Wellington Quigley | Capistrano Beach, California, United States | PHOTOGRAPHER: UNDINE PRÖHL

On occasions, the times in which we live contribute to the creation of coastal architecture as something ephemeral, changeable, and provisional. All of this, fruit of a culture based on image, fantasy, and visual references, which strongly wagers on spontaneity, is used to attract tourism and economic growth in a particular area. As with authentic settings, this type of architecture becomes a point of reference that is copied to fulfill collective fantasies that, for contrast, mankind situates alongside examples of natural beauty. Capistrano Beach is a place on the California coast that is character-ized by a proliferation of single-family residences along the seafront, built directly over the sand in a harsh paradoxical architectural complex that is full of juxtapositions, tensions, and fragments that make up a final unit, which can truly only be read by a visit to the area itself. This house is composed of two parallel planes, the east and west supporting walls. On the north and south faces, these planes dematerialize and allow for an interaction between interior and exterior. In these two facades, the lines used are gently curved and bring the naturally eroded landscape into evidence.

HOUSE TERRACE OVER THE SAND OF THE BEACH

In recognition of the beauty of the beach's different areas, the house was designed as an uncomplicated volumetric composition, which is made up of fragments and successions that refer to a variety of styles. The visual reading of the different elements conveys an architecture that offers different depths of significance and produces ambiguity and tension. The street side of the house is characterized by volumetric segregation and differentiation that blur the limits between this house and the neighboring houses. Nothing more than the path and a light offer the clues necessary to reconstruct a complete understanding of the architectural experience. In its privileged location, the architecture of this residence tends toward a form of hedonism that is felt within its spaces. Toward the beach, the materials adapt to an architecture that is more mobile, less rigid, and more in keeping with the sun and bathing environment at the water's edge.

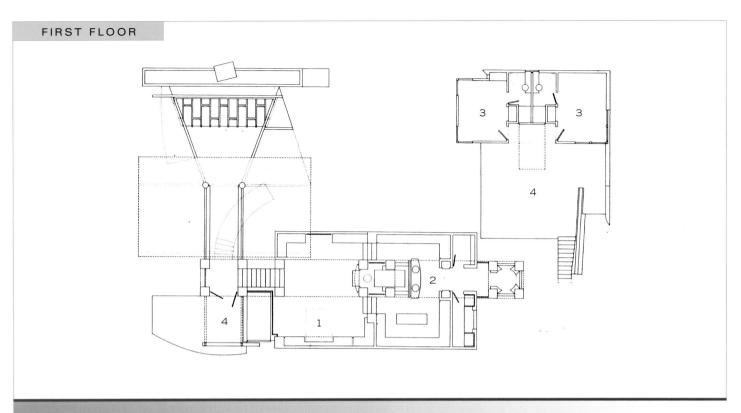

1. MASTER BEDROOM	5. ENTRANCE	9. SOFA ZONE
2. MAIN BATHROOM	6. FLOWER BED	10. DINING ROOM
3. GUEST ROOM	7. GARAGE	11. KITCHEN
4. TERRACE	8. LIVING ROOM	12. BATHROOM

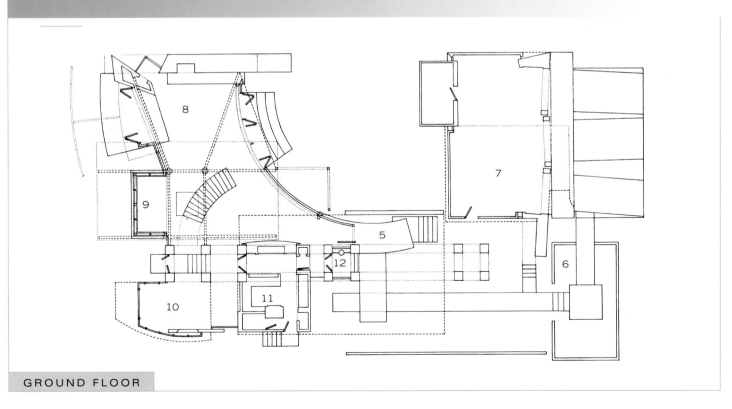

GROUND FLOOR

Daily life is carried out in the ground floor interior space, which is characterized by the way the walls and their textures have been treated in order to capture the light. On the exterior, the vegetation takes on the role of a final covering along with the varied range of materials used for this purpose.

The single curved flight of stairs leads to the bedroom area, bathroom, study, and guest apartment on the upper floor.

CABO SAN LUCAS HOUSE

Steven Harris Architects | Cabo San Lucas, Baja California Sur, Mexico | PHOTOGRAPHERS: MARK DARLEY (VIEW), ANTONIO ZANINOVIC

On the southern tip of Baja California, Cabo San Lucas, where the desert meets the sea in a landscape characterized by bushes and cacti but little green vegetation, a precipice more than seventy-five meters high looks out onto the Pacific Ocean. In this place, between the sea and the desert, Steven Harris Architects constructed a house in which the relationship of the residence to the landscape is the project's main focus. With this in mind, the house is set into various sections situated around the perimeter of the plot. These do not come into contact with the central space, which was consequently converted into a large patio that is open to the landscape, whose vegetation and the preexisting rock formations have been retained. In this way, the dialogue continues between the landscape and the house where the interiors have different spatial relationships with their settings, ranging from rooms excavated into the bedrock to others suspended on the edge of the cliff face. All of the elements of the residence are conceived "with an austerity and abstract geometry that contrasts with the extravagant rocks of the setting."

The steep incline of the plot led to positioning the different parts of the house on the site in a series of levels according to how it was excavated, and always around the large patio up to the cliffs, from which the views of the sea and the sky become overpowering.

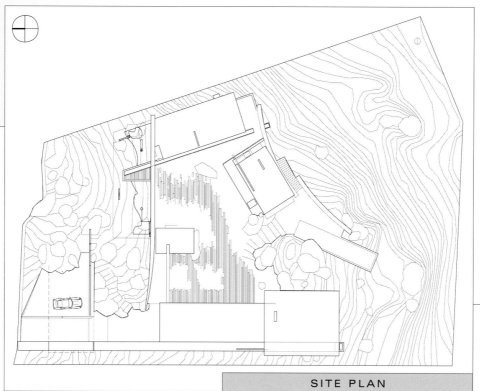

SITE PLAN

Going down in a southerly direction from highway level, the roofs of the different sections of the house can be seen. The access to the house is found in the upper part of the plot, where the first section of the complex is located. It contains the garage and the ramp, between stone walls, to the porch that indicates the entrance to the patio area. This space, irregular in shape, opens onto the sea, framed by the different sections of the house, which protect it from the view of neighboring properties. The east section of the patio is where the private spaces of the house, such as the bedrooms and the studio, are situated. The west part of the patio contains the public spaces and the service quarters. Buried in the hill on the northern face is a section that accommodates the audio-video room and the gym. This leaves the southern area of the patio, limited by the two retaining walls faced in stone that, on the edge of the cliff face, support the outside living room and, on a lower level, the swimming pool.

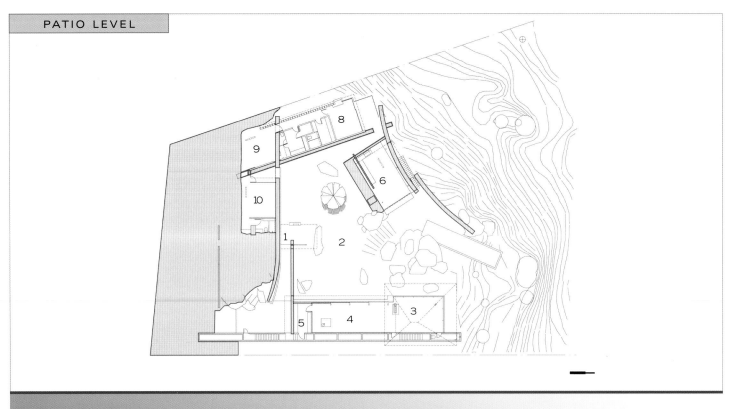

1. ENTRANCE
2. PATIO
3. LIVING ROOM
4. DINING ROOM
5. KITCHEN
6. TERRACE
7. SWIMMING POOL
8. BEDROOM
9. GYM
10. AUDIO-VIDEO ROOM
11. STUDY
12. SERVICE AREA

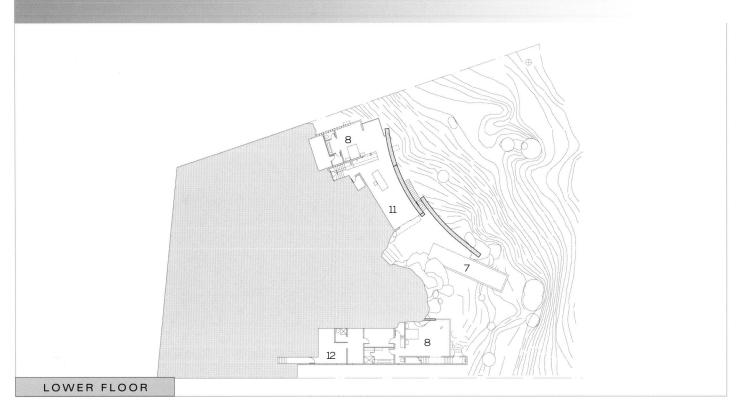

LOWER FLOOR

Alongside the retaining walls, faced in local stone, the other vertical decorative elements have been painted white and in a brown that complements the colors of the soil and rocks of the area, another example of the search for a dialog between house and landscape.

The structure of the house is based on steel-reinforced concrete used in a conventional way in order to coincide with the technologies and knowledge of the local work force.

CROSS SECTION

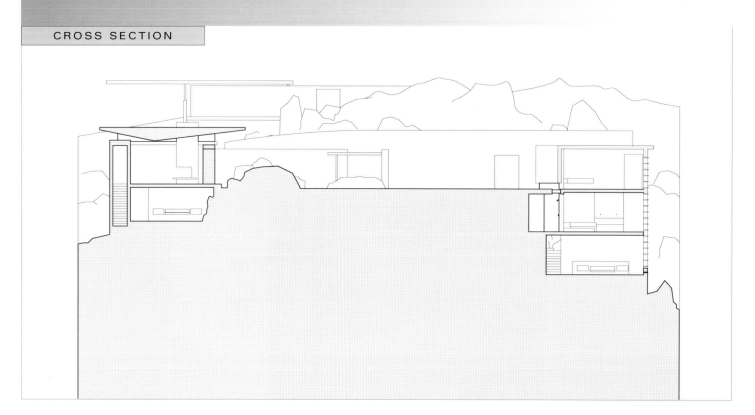

In the clean openings, a highly resistant laminated glass was used with an anchoring system calculated to withstand the force of the hurricanes that periodically occur in the area. In this way, it was possible to glaze much larger areas than if habitual systems had been used.

The interior flooring is gray concrete to complement the local stone that was used for all of the paving and facings in the patio.

SECTION ACROSS LENGTH

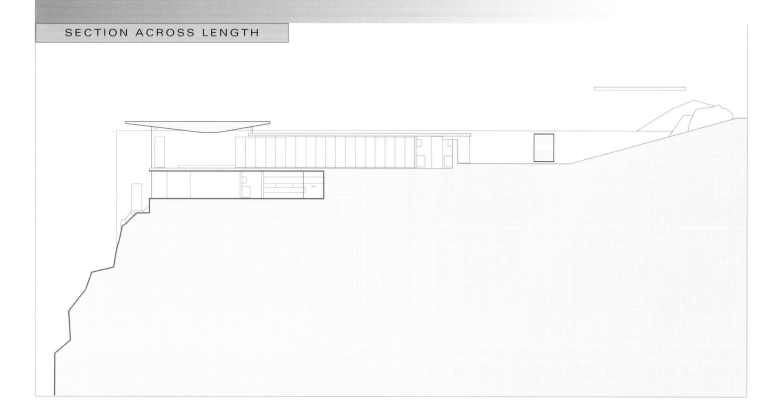

The house is an excellent example of how abstract architecture shaped by constant dialog with its surroundings can become well integrated within a landscape.

CASA IXTAPA

Fernando Romero-LCM | Ixtapa, Guerrero, Mexico | PHOTOGRAPHERS: PAUL CZITROM, LUIS GORDOA

Punta Ixtapa is a lovely place on the Pacific coast of Mexico where an optimum balance between new construction and the natural surroundings has been preserved. The climate is tropical and the area receives strong sun and abundant rain, which have shaped the hills, covered in dense vegetation that hangs over the ocean. Here, behind one of the private beaches that overlook the Pacific Ocean, Fernando Romero has designed a "continuous surface folded back upon itself" as a second residence for a large family who wanted to be able to get together in the area of Guerrero.

Because of the strict regulations in this urban area, buildings must be constructed "in a traditional style," which means that local stone and the traditional colors of the area have to be used, along with *palapa* (the traditional palm-leaf roofing of the region). This factor had an enormous influence on the architecture of this house by the sea in the tropics, and it reflects the organic architecture of the twentieth century.

The house "comes out of a single surface which, being folded back upon itself, defines the differences between the public and private spaces" and separates functions by floors. As a result, the public areas, alongside the parents' bedroom, have been situated downstairs, while the rest of the family's bedrooms and the guest room are on the upper floor.

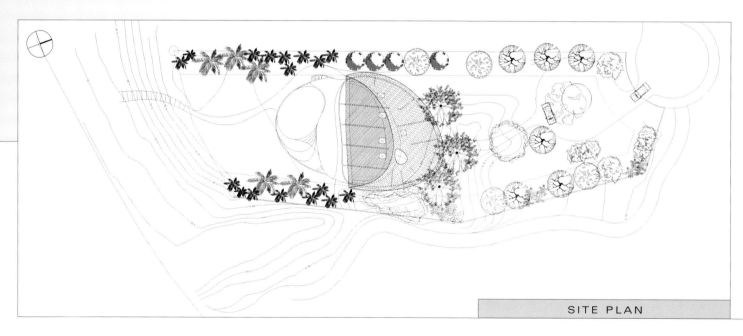

SITE PLAN

The entrance to the house is at the end of a long, winding drive that, upon reaching the curved walls of the ground floor and crossing the threshold, runs into an impressive open-air living/dining area. This exterior space makes the most of the warm weather enjoyed throughout the year and opens out directly onto the landscape. It was conceived as an immense space in which the entire family could get together. The living/dining area constitutes the beginning of a splendid succession of exterior spaces that run from the large porch of the living area and continue across the terrace, around the swimming pool, through the garden, finally reaching the beach and the Pacific Ocean.

Situated around the exterior living area we find the staircase that leads to the kitchen, a lavatory, the inside living room (or storm retreat), and the parents' bedroom. The rest of the bedrooms can be accessed by going upstairs, among the curves of the curious landing area.

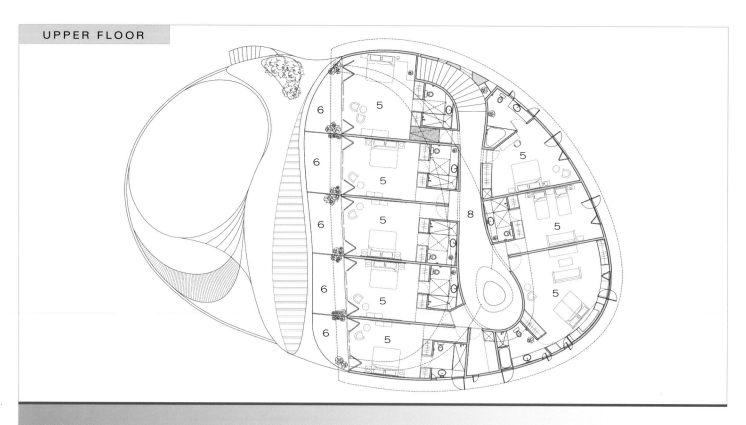

1. ENTRANCE
2. LIVING / DINING AREA

3. KITCHEN
4. "STORM RETREAT"

5. BEDROOM
6. TERRACE

7. SWIMMING POOL
8. LANDING

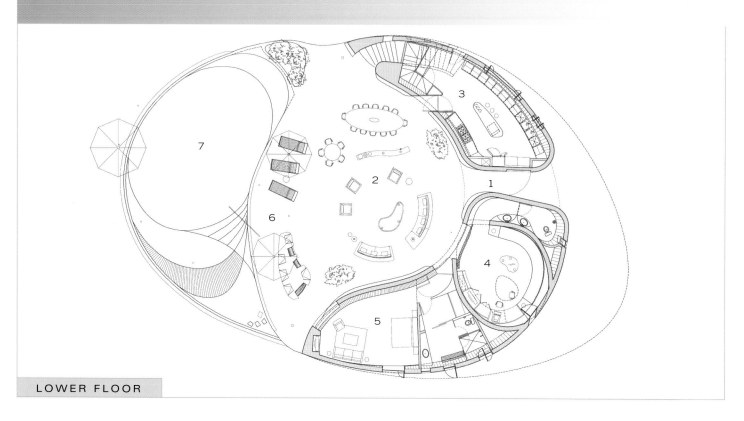

The large porch without pillars in the exterior living area, the vaults, and the sinuous curves that make up the house are possible due to the structure of steel-reinforced concrete.

The structure of the steel-reinforced concrete accompanied by the vertical ornamental curves in white-covered brick, along with the light-colored floors, produce the abstract interior spaces.

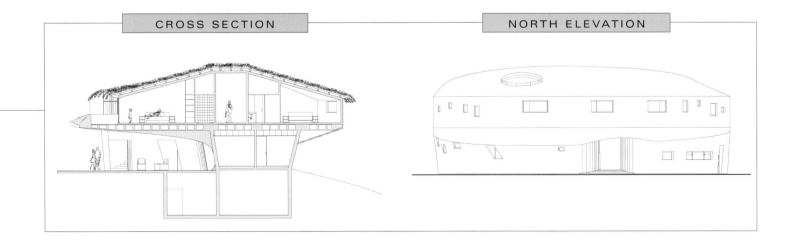

CROSS SECTION

NORTH ELEVATION

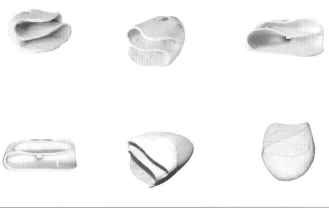

"The scheme is based on the idea of a unique surface folded back upon itself," which makes up a house "designed in such a way that a large family can enjoy days of beach and contemplation in a remarkable place."

CASA NA PRAIA FELIX

Anne Marie Summer | Ubatuba, São Paulo, Brazil | PHOTOGRAPHER: NELSON KON

While the beach of Felix overlooks the sea, the exuberant vegetation of the "Atlantic undergrowth" touches its back. Amidst this jungle and looking toward the Atlantic Ocean from the hills of the Brazilian province of Ubatuba, the architect Anne Marie Summer has built a "floating terrace" that rises above the treetops to overlook the sea and manifest itself as a blue spot in the green landscape. This is a house to see and to see from, as its interiors and exteriors are intimately related.

The house synthesizes formally as a horizontal plane that looks out over the landscape while occupying a pronounced gradient and creating two volumes, each consisting of one floor. The higher area is anchored to the hill, where it opens onto a terrace, and the lower has a terrace on its roof and is supported by a vertical plane held up by the spine of the topography. The architectural language used is both bold and respectful of its location and neighbors.

SITE PLAN

Supported by the steep gradient of the hill, the house consists of two floors. On the upper floor, the access, established over a large terrace or "open-air plaza," allows enjoyment of the area's impressive views. Behind this, and anchored in the terrain, we find the kitchen, the living/dining room, a lavatory, and the service area, while the four bedrooms and their respective bathrooms are located on the lower floor. The bedrooms are reached across two lateral porches that also serve as terraces for the bedrooms. The two floors are joined by two staircases: an interior one, diagonal to the two spaces it connects, and an exterior one, which links the upper terrace with the two porches on the lower floor.

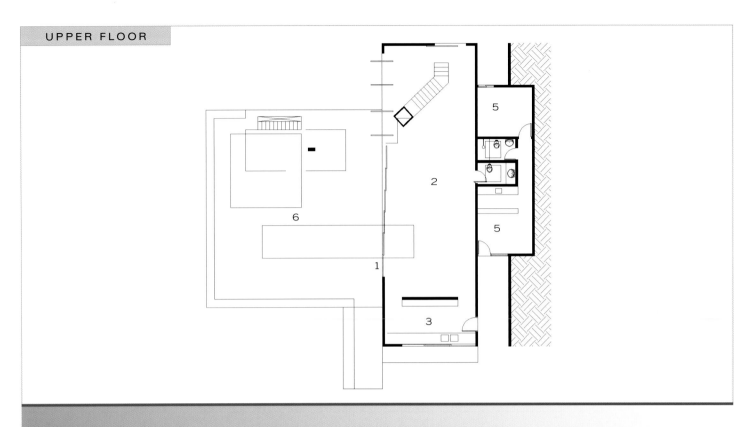

1. ENTRANCE
2. LIVING / DINING ROOM
3. KITCHEN

4. BEDROOM
5. SERVICE RESIDENCE
6. TERRACE

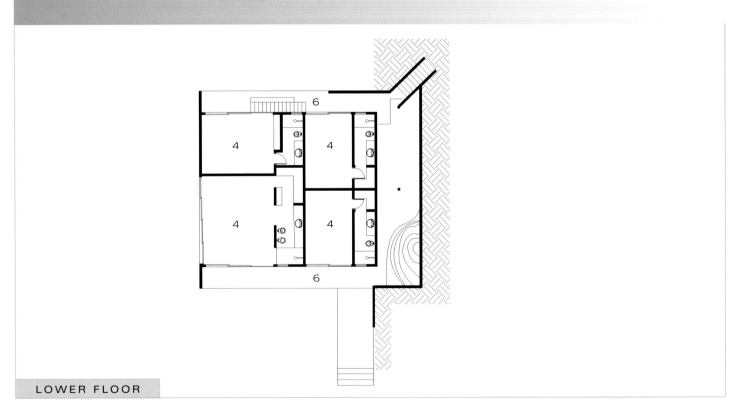

The color scheme of interior white and exterior blue is not repeated in the flooring. Both the inside and outside areas are paved in "Portuguese mosaic," which combines dark basalt with creams of limestone and creates coherence in this house, in which the interior becomes part of the exterior.

Wood was used only in the carpentry of the windows and for the long bench that also serves as a balustrade for the large terrace.

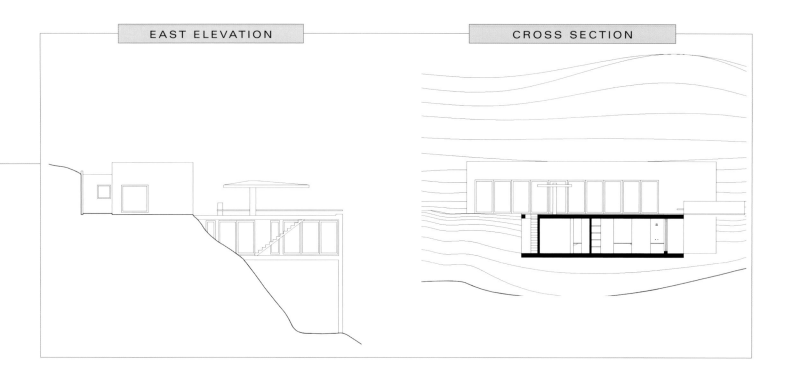

EAST ELEVATION

CROSS SECTION

All of the exterior walls have been painted in a particular blue that causes the house to stand out as a blue tint in the landscape.

CASA X

Barclay & Crousse | "La Escondida" Beach, Cañete, Peru | PHOTOGRAPHER: JEAN PIERRE CROUSSE

On the Peruvian coast, where one of the most arid deserts in the world meets the Pacific Ocean, the extreme fluctuations in temperature and the low levels of humidity of the desert climate are regulated by the existence of the vast ocean. This encounter of climate and landscape, these two infinite voids of sea and desert that come face to face on the coastline, led the architects to conceive a shelter on a human scale in a hollow in the area—a house that offers the intimacy necessary to both live in the desert and contemplate the sea.

On this site, with neither rain nor wind, the comfortable average temperature—oscillating between 59°F (15°C) in the winter and 84°F (29°C) in the summer—and the almost imperceptible variation between day and night due to high humidity in the atmosphere make

protection from the tropical sun the only physical condition necessary for living here. "To achieve this aim, we opted for a double strategy on the project. We aimed, first, for the maximum use of the space available for building on the plot and, second, to define this space by a solid form that was more than simply the volumetric limit we should construct. As a result, a pure prism came about, stranded in the dunes and giving the impression of always having been there. This preexisting solid was later excavated throughout the design process that extracted material so as to simultaneously create and discover its spaces, similar to how archeologists dug away the sand and discovered pre-Columbian ruins buried by the passage of time."

The formal logic of the house, the act of "taking away matter," which is contrary to the typical logic of construction, was applied to

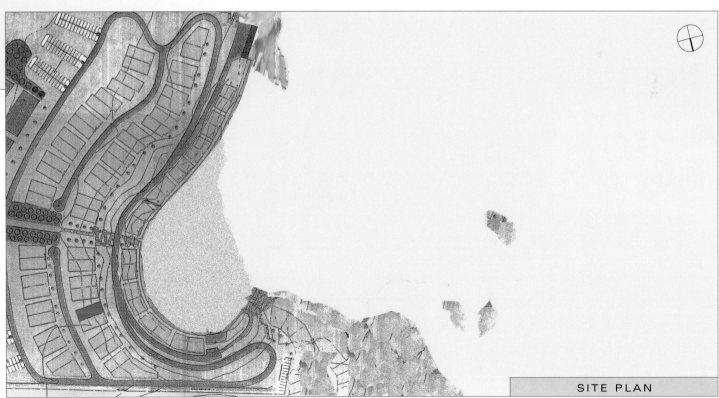

all aspects of the project. This led to the production of a succession of interior/exterior spaces classified by their differing relationships with the sky and the sea. Following the lay of the land, Casa X presents two levels: the upper, where all of the nonprivate spaces of the residence are located, and the lower, where the bedrooms are found.

The access to the house is across a threshold that separates two exterior spaces—the infinite space of the desert and the intimate space of the entrance patio. This patio goes on toward the ocean along a large terrace, like an artificial beach that relates to the sea and its horizon by means of a long, narrow swimming pool. The roofing, conceived as a large horizontal plane that spans the width of

the plot, frames the seascape and shelters the living/dining room as would a beach umbrella. In this way, the limits between the room and the terrace disappear, thanks to a sliding glass partition. The staircase, situated outside and following the gradient of the land, unifies the upper level with the bedrooms, which are located below a large terrace, while a space protected from the sun by the wooden slats of the terrace flooring provides access to the children's bedroom and the guest room. At the end of the staircase, across from a porch situated just below the swimming pool overlooking the ocean, is the master bedroom.

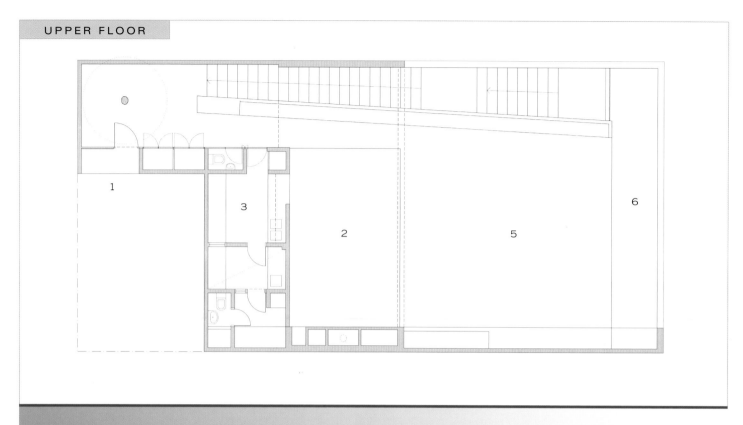

1. ENTRANCE
2. LIVING /DINING ROOM
3. KITCHEN

4. BEDROOM
5. TERRACE
6. SWIMMING POOL

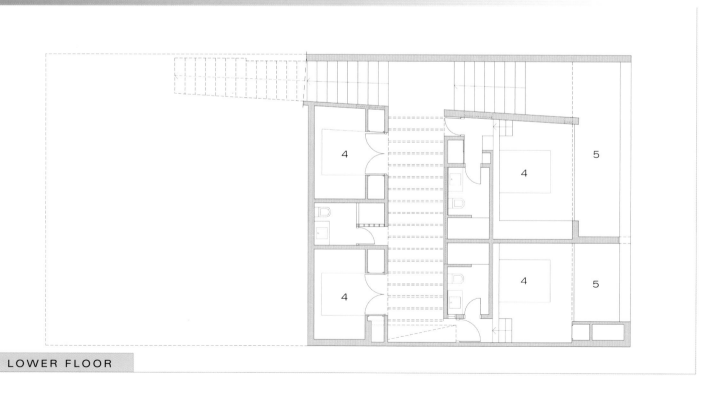

The great travel time between the Peruvian site and the architects' Paris office obliged a rationalization of the building systems and a reduction of details to the most essential, so that they could be undertaken by local labor without direct supervision.

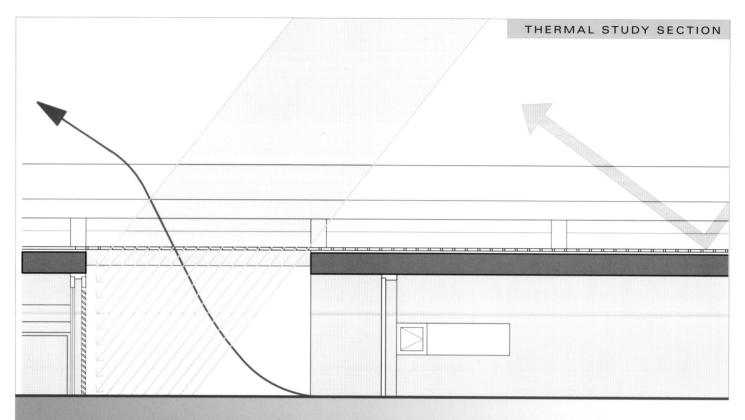

When it came to establishing the interior spaces, the warm climate and the small amount of rainfall meant that the essential condition factors were protection from the sun and control of the warm sea breezes.

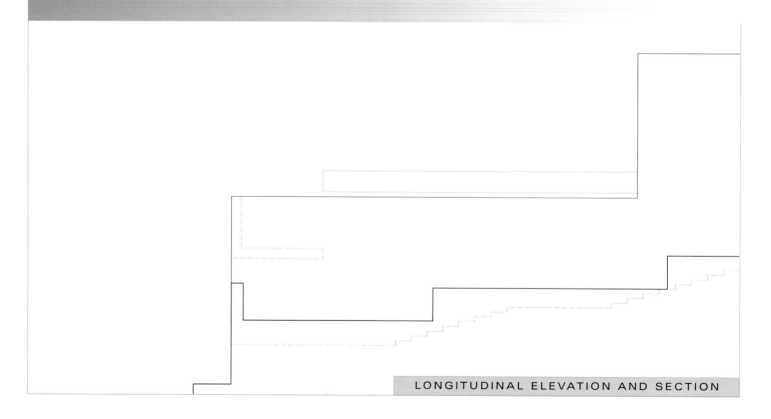

LONGITUDINAL ELEVATION AND SECTION

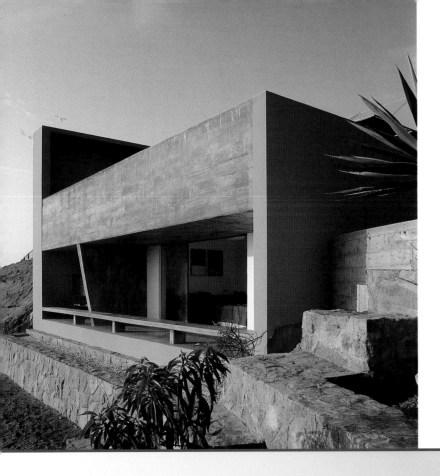

The interiors of the house combine white and red with the omnipresent sandy ocher color. This color, which avoids the "visual aging of the building" because of the dust that is transported by the desert winds, harmonizes well with the color scheme established by both the wood and the concrete paving.

"The process of excavating the volume of the house produced spaces delineated by enclosures in which the ambiguity between the closed and open spaces has been intensified maximally and, in this way, expressed by their differing relationships with the sky or with the sea."

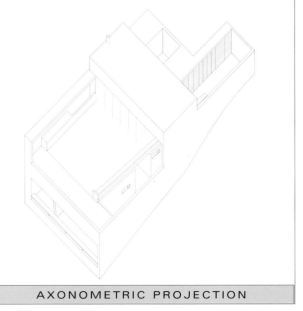

AXONOMETRIC PROJECTION

From the outside, the ocher color reaffirms the unity between the house and its landscape.

Editor, English-language edition: Dorothy Fink
Designer, English-language edition: Shawn Dahl
Jacket design, English-language edition: Neil Egan
Production Manager, English-language edition: Jacquie Poirier

Library of Congress Control Number: 2006939105

ISBN 10: 0-8109-9296-5
ISBN 13: 9-780-8109-9296-2

Originally published in Spanish under the title *Casas junto al mar* by
Atrium Group, Barcelona, 2004.

Copyright © 2004 Atrium Group de Ediciones y Publicaciones, S.L.,
Barcelona
English translation copyright © 2007 Abrams, New York

Printed and bound in China
10 9 8 7 6 5 4 3 2 1

HNA
harry n. abrams, inc.
a subsidiary of La Martinière Groupe
115 West 18th Street
New York, NY 10011
www.hnabooks.com